A Treatise on the Pāramīs

From the Commentary to
the Cariyāpiṭaka

Ācariya Dhammapāla

Translated from the Pāli by
Bhikkhu Bodhi

Buddhist Publication Society
Kandy • Sri Lanka

Published in 1996

Buddhist Publication Society
P.O. Box 61
54, Sangharaja Mawatha
Kandy, Sri Lanka

Excerpted from *The Discourse on the All-Embracing Net of Views: The Brahmajāla Sutta and Its Commentaries*. Copyright © 1978 by Bhikkhu Bodhi.

ISBN 955-24-0146-1

Typeset at the BPS
Text set in Times

Printed in Sri Lanka by
Karunaratne & Sons Ltd.
Colombo 10

THE WHEEL PUBLICATION 409/411

Introduction

In its earliest phase, as represented by the four main collections of the Sutta Piṭaka, the focal concern of Buddhism was the attainment of nibbāna by the practice of the Noble Eightfold Path. In these collections the Buddha teaches his doctrine as a direct path to deliverance, and perhaps no feature of the presentation is so striking as the urgency he enjoins on his disciples in bringing their spiritual work to completion by reaching the final goal. Just as a man who discovers his turban to be in flames would immediately seek to extinguish it, so should the earnest disciple strive to extinguish the flames of craving in order to reach the state of security, the consummate peace of nibbāna.

The oldest suttas, however, already mention three types of individuals who attain to the consummate state: a *sammāsambuddha* or perfectly enlightened Buddha, who realizes the goal without the aid of a teacher and teaches the Dhamma to others, founding a dispensation (*sāsana*); a *paccekabuddha* or solitary enlightened one, who achieves realization unaided but does not establish a dispensation; and a disciple *arahat*, who realizes the goal through the instruction of a supreme Buddha and then teaches others according to his inclination and capacity. With the passage of time, quite possibly due to a decline in practice and an increasing rarity of higher attainments, these three types came to be viewed as three alternative ideals towards which a disciple could aspire in the hope of some distant future attainment. All were identical in their realization of nibbāna, but each was seen to stand for a distinct aspect of the enlightened personality and to presuppose a distinct *yāna*, a "vehicle" or spiritual career, leading to its actualization. For the Theravāda, the more conservative of the ancient schools, the emphasis was always placed on the ideal prescribed in the Pāli suttas, the attainment of arahatship by following the instructions of the historical Buddha; the other ideals remained in the background, acknowledged but not especially attended to. Other early schools, such as the Sarvāstivāda and the Mahāsaṅghika, while upholding the primacy of the disciple's course and the arahat ideal, also gave consideration to the other ideals as possible goals for individuals inclined to pursue them. Thus they came to admit a doctrine of three *yānas* or vehicles to deliverance, all valid but steeply graded in difficulty and accessibility.

Within all the early schools, thinkers and poets alike attempted to fill in the background history to the three enlightened persons, composing stories of their past lives in which they prepared the foundations for their future achievements. Since it was the figure of the Buddha, as the founder of the Dispensation, who commanded the greatest awe and veneration, gradually a literature began to emerge depicting the evolution of the bodhisattva or "Buddha-to-be" along the arduous path of his development. In this way the figure of the bodhisattva,* the aspirant to Buddhahood, came to claim an increasingly prominent place in the popular Buddhist religious life. The culmination of these innovations was the appearance, in about the first century B.C., of the Mahāyāna, the self-styled "Great Vehicle," which proclaimed that of the three vehicles to enlightenment the bodhisattva-vehicle was alone ultimate, the other two being only expedients devised by the Buddha to lead his less competent disciples to perfect Buddhahood, which they held to be the only valid spiritual ideal.

Through its conservative bent and relative insulation from the other schools, the Theravāda managed to resist the metamorphic changes taking place elsewhere in the Buddhist world, preserving the teachings as compiled at the early councils without radical alterations of their doctrinal framework. Nevertheless, in this school as well, from a period even preceding the rise of the Mahāyāna, the figure of the bodhisattva began to make inroads into both its litera-

---

* Here and throughout I use the Sanskrit word in preference to the less familiar Pāli "bodhisatta."

ture and spiritual atmosphere. Two elements in the early teaching seem to have provided the germs for this development. One was the fact that the Buddha had used the word "bodhisattva" to refer to himself in the period preceding his enlightenment, pushing its scope as far back as his existence in the Tusita heaven before his final descent to earth. The second was the recognition of the multiplicity of Buddhas, which showed the Sakyan Gotama to be, not a unique figure in the cosmic genealogy, but only the most recent member of a series of Buddhas each of whom attains enlightenment, founds a dispensation, and liberates a multitude of beings from the bondage of saṁsāric suffering. The Dīgha Nikāya mentions by name the six most recent predecessors of the Buddha Gotama (D.ii,2), and predicts as well the advent of Metteyya, the Buddha of the future, who will rekindle the lamp of the true Dhamma after it is extinguished in the dark ages that lie ahead (D.iii,76).

These two features jointly implied the existence of "germinal Buddhas" or bodhisattvas toiling to perfect themselves through countless lives in order to reach the summit of supreme enlightenment. The trials and triumphs of the being who became our own Buddha were recorded in the Jātaka tales, relating the bodhisattva's conduct in his previous births. Just when and how the bodhisattva entered upon this course is told in the *Buddhavaṁsa*, a late addition to the Sutta Piṭaka, in a story which has become the paradigm for all subsequent developments of the bodhisattva ideal. According to this story, incalculable aeons ago in the far distant past, our bodhisattva (as the ascetic Sumedha) made an aspiration (*abhinīhāra*) at the feet of the Buddha Dīpankara, the twenty-fourth Buddha of antiquity, in which he renounced the right to enter nibbāna then open to him, in order that he might become a Buddha in the future and provide salvation for the host of gods and humans. He then received a prediction from the Buddha confirming his future success, went off into solitude, and reflected on the qualities that had to be perfected to fulfil his goal. These, the ten *pāramīs*, became the standard constituents of the bodhisattva's practice, the "requisites of enlightenment" (*bodhisambhāra*) of our present treatise.

But though the existence of a bodhisattva career was thus acknowledged by the Theravāda, the dominant attitude prevailed among the exponents of the school that this path was reserved only for the very rare and exceptional individual. Since it was not recommended in the oldest authentic records of the Buddha's teaching, those who professed to follow the Buddha were advised to comply with the instructions contained in these documents and aim at the attainment of nibbāna by the practice of the Noble Eightfold Path. Thus the bulk of literature in the Pāli school was devoted to explaining the details of this path and its doctrinal ramifications, while the practice of the pāramīs was treated only in broad and general terms.

As time passed, however, perhaps partly through the influence of the Mahāyāna, the bodhisattva ideal must have come to acquire an increasing appeal for the minds of the Buddhist populace, and the need became felt for a work explaining in a practical manner the factors and phases of the *pāramitā* path without deviating from the established doctrinal position of the Theravāda. Works expounding the bodhisattva career abounded in the Mahāyāna schools, since this was their axial concern, but a comparable work was lacking in Theravāda circles. To meet this need, apparently, Ācariya Dhammapāla composed his "Treatise on the Pāramīs," which is found in at least two places in the Pāli exegetical literature, in a complete version in the Cariyāpiṭaka Aṭṭhakathā, and in an abridged version in the *ṭīkā* or subcommentary to the Brahmajāla Sutta.

The work introduces itself as a treatise composed "for clansmen following the suttas who are zealously engaged in the practice of the vehicle to great enlightenment, in order to improve their skilfulness in accumulating the requisites of enlightenment." Followers of the suttas (*suttantikas*) are specified probably because those who aspired to follow the bodhisattva course had to work selectively from various suttas to determine the practices appropriate for their aim, as the text itself illustrates in filling out its material. The mention of the "vehicle to great enlightenment" (*mahābodhiyāna*) does not indicate the historical Mahāyāna, but signifies rather the greatness of the bodhisattva career by reason of the loftiness of its goal and its capacity to provide for the emancipation of a great number of beings.

The "requisites of enlightenment" are the pāramīs themselves, the main topic of the treatise. The word *pāramī* derives from *parama*, "supreme," and thus suggests the eminence of the qualities which must be fulfilled by a bodhisattva in the long course of his spiritual development. But the cognate *pāramitā*, the word preferred by the Mahāyāna texts and also used by Pāli writers, is sometimes explained as *pāram + ita*, "gone to the beyond," thereby indicating the transcendental direction of these qualities. The list of pāramīs in the Pāli tradition differs somewhat from the more familiar list given in Sanskrit works, which probably antedates the Mahāyāna and provided a ready set of categories for its use. Our author shows that the two lists can be correlated in section xii, and the coincidence of a number of items points to a central core already forming before the two traditions went their separate ways. The six pāramīs of the Sanskrit heritage are: giving, virtue, patience, energy, meditation, and wisdom. Later Mahāyāna texts add four more—resolution, skilful means, power, and knowledge—in order to co-ordinate on a one-to-one basis the list of perfections with the account of the ten stages of the bodhisattva's ascent to Buddhahood. The Pāli works, including those composed before the rise of Mahāyāna, give a different though partly overlapping list of ten: giving, virtue, renunciation, wisdom, energy, patience, truthfulness, determination, loving-kindness, and equanimity. Unlike the Mahāyāna, the Theravāda never developed a theory of stages, though such may be implicit in the grading of the pāramīs into three degrees as basic, intermediate, and ultimate (section xi).

The treatise draws upon various sources for its material, both Theravāda and Mahāyāna, and thus represents perhaps a unique instance of a classical style Theravāda work consciously borrowing from its northern cousin; in matters of philosophical doctrine, however, the work never deviates from the Theravāda perspective. The set of ten pāramīs itself comes from the *Buddhavaṁsa*, as does the discussion of the great aspiration (*abhinīhāra*) with its eight qualifications. All of this had become part of the standard Theravāda tradition by the time the work was composed and was easily absorbed. Other Pāli sources—the suttas, Jātakas, later canonical works, the *Visuddhimagga*, etc.—have all contributed to the overall composition of the treatise. The basic methodology of the commentaries is evident in the explication of the ten pāramīs by way of the fourfold defining device of characteristic, function, manifestation, and proximate cause (section v). The heritage of the oral traditions of various teachers in later Pāli scholasticism is seen in the various views expressed on the three grades of practice for each pāramī (section xi), on the correlation of the four foundations with the different stages of the bodhisattva's career (section xii), and on the classification of time required for the completion of the pāramīs (section xiv). Perhaps the influence of another early school, the Sarvāstivāda, lies behind the dyadic treatment of the six pāramītas (section xii).

The main Mahāyāna work utilized by the author is the *Bodhisattvabhūmi*, the fifteenth chapter of the *Yogācārabhūmi*, a voluminous text of the Yogācāra school ascribed to Maitreyanātha, the teacher of Asanga. The *Bodhisattvabhūmi* has contributed to the sections on the practice of the pāramīs, particularly the first, on the four shackles to giving, and on the special accomplishments resulting from the pāramīs. The originals, however, have all been divested of their specifically Mahāyāna features to make them fully compatible with the Theravāda perspective. Mahāyāna influence may further be discernible in the emphasis on compassion and skilful means, in the vows to benefit all beings, in the statement that the bodhisattva causes beings "to enter and reach maturity in the three vehicles," etc.

On points of doctrine, as we mentioned, the work remains well within the bounds of Theravāda orthodoxy. Its section on the perfection of wisdom has nothing more in common with the

Prajñāpāramitā literature than the core of Buddhist doctrine shared by all schools. There is nothing about the identity of nibbāna and saṁsāra, the triple body of the Buddha, the suchness and sameness of all dhammas, mind-only, the provisional nature of the disciple and paccekabuddha vehicles, or any of the other ideas distinctive of the Mahāyāna. Even the mention of emptiness (*suññatā*) is restricted to the absence of a self or ego-entity and is not carried through to the radical ontology of the Mahāyāna sūtras. The discussion of wisdom draws entirely upon the Pāli suttas and the *Visuddhimagga*, only with the stipulation that the bodhisattva must balance wisdom with compassion and skilful means and must postpone his entrance upon the supramundane path until his requisites of enlightenment are fully mature.

It should be noted that in established Theravāda tradition the pāramīs are not regarded as a discipline peculiar to candidates for Buddhahood alone but as practices which must be fulfilled by all aspirants to enlightenment and deliverance, whether as Buddhas, paccekabuddhas, or disciples. What distinguishes the supreme bodhisattva from aspirants in the other two vehicles is the degree to which the pāramīs must be cultivated and the length of time they must be pursued. But the qualities themselves are universal requisites for deliverance, which all must fulfil to at least a minimal degree to merit the fruits of the liberating path.

The present translation has been based on the version in the Cariyāpiṭaka Aṭṭhakathā, in the Burmese-script Sixth Council edition. This has been abridged in places in deference to the size limits of a Wheel booklet. For a translation of the complete text, the reader is directed to my translation of the Brahmajāla Sutta and its commentaries, *The Discourse on the All-Embracing Net of Views* (BPS 1978, 1992), Part IV.

BHIKKHU BODHI

A Treatise on the Pāramīs

We now undertake a detailed explanation of the pāramīs for clansmen following the suttas who are zealously engaged in the practice of the vehicle to great enlightenment (*mahābodhiyāna*), in order to improve their skilfulness in accumulating the requisites for enlightenment.

This is the schedule of the questions: (i) What are the pāramīs? (ii) In what sense are they called pāramīs? (iii) How many are there? (iv) What is their sequence? (v) What are their characteristics, functions, manifestations, and proximate causes? (vi) What is their condition? (vii) What is their defilement? (viii) What is their cleansing? (ix) What are their opposites? (x) How are they to be practised? (xi) How are they analyzed? (xii) How are they synthesized? (xiii) By what means are they accomplished? (xiv) How much time is required to accomplish them? (xv) What benefits do they bring? (xvi) What is their fruit? The answers follow.

(i) WHAT ARE THE PĀRAMĪS?

The pāramīs are the noble qualities such as giving, etc., accompanied by compassion and skilful means, and untainted by craving, conceit, and views.[1]

(ii) IN WHAT SENSE ARE THEY CALLED "PĀRAMĪS"?

The bodhisattvas, the great beings, are supreme (*parama*), since they are the highest of beings by reason of their distinguished qualities such as giving, virtue, etc. The pāramīs—the activities of giving, etc.—are their character or their conduct. Or else: he excels, thus he is supreme (*paratī ti paramo*). The bodhisattva is the fulfiller and guardian of the noble qualities such as giving, etc.; that which belongs to the supreme—the character or conduct of the one who is supreme (i.e. of the bodhisattva)—is a pāramī, i.e. the activities of giving, etc.

(iii) HOW MANY ARE THERE?

In brief there are ten. These have come down in the texts in their specific character. As it is said:

> "How many qualities are there, Lord, issuing in Buddhahood?"
> "There are, Sāriputta, ten qualities issuing in Buddhahood. What are the ten? Giving, Sāriputta, is a quality issuing in Buddhahood. Virtue, renunciation, wisdom, energy, patience, truthfulness, determination, loving-kindness, and equanimity are qualities issuing in Buddhahood."[2]

But some say there are six. This is said by way of their synthesis, which we will explain below (section xii).

(iv) WHAT IS THEIR SEQUENCE?

Here "sequence" means sequence of teaching. This sequence is rooted in the order in which the pāramīs are initially undertaken, which in turn is rooted in the order in which they are investigated.[3] The quality which is investigated and undertaken at the beginning is taught first. Therein, giving is stated first, for giving assists (the development of) virtue and is easy to practise. Giving accompanied by virtue is abundantly fruitful and beneficial, so virtue is stated immediately after giving. Virtue accompanied by renunciation... renunciation by wisdom ... wisdom by energy ... energy by patience ... patience by truthfulness ... truthfulness by determination ... determination by loving-kindness ... and loving-kindness accompanied by equanimity is abundantly fruitful and beneficial; thus equanimity is stated immediately after loving-kindness. Equanimity is accompanied by compassion and compassion by equanimity. (Someone may ask:) "How can the bodhisattvas, the great compassionate ones, look upon living beings with equanimity?" Some teachers say: "Sometimes they show equanimity towards living beings when it is necessary to do so." But others say: "They do not show equanimity towards living beings (as such), but towards the offensive actions performed by beings."

Another method (of explaining the sequence) may be given:

(1) *Giving* is stated at the beginning: (a) because it is common to all beings, since even ordinary people practise giving; (b) because it is the least fruitful; and (c) because it is the easiest to practise.

(2) *Virtue* is stated immediately after giving: (a) because virtue purifies both the donor and the recipient; (b) to show that, while giving benefits others, virtue prevents the affliction of others; (c) in order to state a factor of abstinence immediately after a factor of positive activity; and (d) in order to show the cause for the achievement of a favourable state of future existence right after the cause for the achievement of wealth.[4]

(3) *Renunciation* is mentioned immediately after virtue: (a) because renunciation perfects the achievement of virtue; (b) in order to list good conduct of mind immediately after good conduct of body and speech; (c) because meditation (*jhāna*) succeeds easily for one who has purified his virtue; (d) in order to show that the purification of one's end (*āsaya*) through the abandoning of the offensive mental defilements follows the purification of one's means (*payoga*) by the abandoning of offensive actions; and (e) to state the abandoning of mental obsessions immediately after the abandoning of bodily and verbal transgressions.[5]

(4) *Wisdom* is mentioned immediately after renunciation: (a) because renunciation is perfected and purified by wisdom; (b) to show that there is no wisdom in the absence of meditation (*jhāna*), since concentration is the proximate cause of wisdom and wisdom the manifestation of concentration; (c) in order to list the causal basis for equanimity immediately after the causal basis for serenity; and (d) to show that skilful means in working for the welfare of others springs from meditation directed to their welfare.

(5) *Energy* is stated immediately after wisdom: (a) because the function of wisdom is perfected by the arousing of energy; (b) to

show the miraculous work the bodhisattva undertakes for the welfare of beings after he has reached reflective acquiescence in their emptiness; (c) to state the causal basis for exertion right after the basis for equanimity; and (d) to state the arousing of energy right after the activity of careful consideration, according to the statement: "The activity of those who have carefully considered brings excellent results."

(6) *Patience* is mentioned immediately after energy: (a) because patience is perfected by energy, as it is said: "The energetic man, by arousing his energy, overcomes the suffering imposed by beings and formations"; (b) because patience is an adornment of energy, as it is said: "The patience of the energetic man shines with splendour"; (c) in order to state the causal basis for serenity immediately after the basis for exertion, for restlessness due to excessive activity is abandoned through reflective acquiescence in the Dhamma;[6] (d) in order to show the perseverence of the man of energy, since one who is patient and free from restlessness perseveres in his work; (e) in order to show the absence of craving for rewards in a bodhisattva diligently engaged in activity for the welfare of others, for there is no craving when he reflects on the Dhamma in accordance with actuality; and (f) to show that the bodhisattva must patiently endure the suffering created by others even when he is working to the utmost for their welfare.

(7) *Truthfulness* is stated immediately after patience: (a) because the determination to practise patience continues long through truthfulness; (b) having first mentioned the patient endurance of wrongs inflicted by others, to mention next fidelity to one's word to render them help; (c) in order to show that a bodhisattva who through patience does not vacillate in the face of abuse, through truthful speech does not relinquish (his antagonist); and (d) to show the truthfulness of the knowledge developed through reflective acquiescence in the emptiness of beings.

(8) *Determination* is stated immediately after truthfulness; (a) because truthfulness is perfected by determination, since abstinence (from falsehood) becomes perfect in one whose determination is

unshakeable; (b) having first shown non-deception in speech, to show next unshakeable commitment to one's word, for a bodhisattva devoted to truth proceeds to fulfil his vows of giving, etc., without wavering; and (c) to show, right after the veracity of knowledge, the complete accumulation of the requisites of enlightenment (*bodhisambhāra*); for one who knows things as they really are determines upon the requisites of enlightenment and brings them to completion by refusing to vacillate in the face of their opposites.[7]

(9) *Loving-kindness* is mentioned immediately after determination: (a) because loving-kindness perfects the determination to undertake activity for the welfare of others; (b) in order to list the work of actually providing for the welfare of others right after stating the determination to do so, for "one determined upon the requisites of enlightenment abides in loving-kindness"; and (c) because the undertaking (of activity for the welfare of others) proceeds imperturbably only when determination is unshakeable.

(10) *Equanimity* is mentioned immediately after loving-kindness: (a) because equanimity purifies loving-kindness; (b) in order to show the indifference one must maintain towards the wrongs inflicted by others when one is providing for their welfare; (c) having mentioned the development of loving-kindness, to state next the development of the quality which evolves from it; and (d) to show the bodhisattva's wonderful virtue of remaining impartial even towards those who wish him well.

Thus the sequence of the pāramīs should be understood as explained.

(v) WHAT ARE THEIR CHARACTERISTICS, FUNCTIONS, MANIFESTATIONS, AND PROXIMATE CAUSES?

Firstly, all the pāramīs, without exception, have as their characteristic the benefitting of others; as their function, the rendering of help to others, or not vacillating; as their manifestation, the wish for the welfare of others, or Buddhahood; and as their proximate cause, great compassion, or compassion and skilful means.

Taken separately, the perfection of giving is the volition of relinquishing oneself and one's belongings, accompanied by compassion and skilful means. The perfection of virtue is good conduct of body and speech, accompanied by compassion and skilful means; in denotation, it is the abstinence from what should not be done, the volition to do what should be done, etc. The perfection of renunciation is the act of consciousness which occurs renouncing sense pleasures and existence, preceded by the perception of their inherent unsatisfactoriness and accompanied by compassion and skilful means. The perfection of wisdom is the comprehension of the general and particular characteristics of dhammas, accompanied by compassion and skilful means. The perfection of energy is bodily and mental work for the welfare of others, accompanied by compassion and skilful means. The perfection of patience is the endurance of harm imposed by beings and formations, or the act of consciousness occurring in such a mode, predominated by non-aversion and accompanied by compassion and skilful means. The perfection of truthfulness is non-deceptiveness in speech, analyzed into an abstinence, a volition, etc., accompanied by compassion and skilful means. The perfection of determination is the unshake-able determination to undertake (activity for the good of others), accompanied by compassion and skilful means; or it is the act of consciousness occurring in such a mode. The perfection of loving-kindness is the wish to provide for the welfare and happiness of the world, accompanied by compassion and skilful means; in denotation, it is benevolence. The perfection of equanimity is the attitude of impartiality towards desirable and undesirable beings and formations, dispelling attraction and repulsion, accompanied by compassion and skilful means.

(*On the basis of these definitions, the characteristics, etc., may be stated thus:*)

(1) *Giving* has the characteristic of relinquishing; its function is to dispel greed for things that can be given away; its manifestation is non-attachment, or the achievement of prosperity and a favour-able state of existence; an object that can be relinquished is its proximate cause.

(2) *Virtue* has the characteristic of composing (*sīlana*); co-ordinating (*samādhāna*) and establishing (*patiṭṭhāna*) are also mentioned as its characteristic. Its function is to dispel moral depravity, or its function is blameless conduct; its manifestation is moral purity; shame and moral dread are its proximate cause.

(3) *Renunciation* has the characteristic of departing from sense pleasures and existence; its function is to verify their unsatisfactoriness; its manifestation is the withdrawal from them; a sense of spiritual urgency (*saṁvega*) is its proximate cause.

(4) *Wisdom* has the characteristic of penetrating the real specific nature (of phenomena), or the characteristic of sure penetration, like the penetration of an arrow shot by a skilful archer; its function is to illuminate the objective field, like a lamp; its manifestation is non-confusion, like a guide in a forest; concentration, or the Four (Noble) Truths, is its proximate cause.

(5) *Energy* has the characteristic of striving; its function is to fortify; its manifestation is indefatigability; an occasion for the arousing of energy, or a sense of spiritual urgency, is its proximate cause.

(6) *Patience* has the characteristic of acceptance; its function is to endure the desirable and undesirable; its manifestation is tolerance or non-opposition; seeing things as they really are is its proximate cause.

(7) *Truthfulness* has the characteristic of non-deceptiveness in speech; its function is to verify in accordance with fact; its manifestation is excellence; honesty is its proximate cause.

(8) *Determination* has the characteristic of determining upon the requisites of enlightenment; its function is to overcome their opposites; its manifestation is unshakeableness in that task; the requisites of enlightenment are its proximate cause.

(9) *Loving-kindness* has the characteristic of promoting the welfare (of living beings); its function is to provide for their welfare, or its function is to remove resentment; its manifestation is kindliness; seeing the agreeable side of beings is its proximate cause.

(10) *Equanimity* has the characteristic of promoting the aspect of neutrality; its function is to see things impartially; its manifesta-

tion is the subsiding of attraction and repulsion: reflection upon the fact that all beings inherit the results of their own kamma is its proximate cause.

And here it should be mentioned that accompaniment by compassion and skilful means is the distinguishing feature of the characteristic of each virtue—e.g. of relinquishing in the case of giving, etc. For the virtues such as giving, etc., which occur in the mental continuities of bodhisattvas are always accompanied by compassion and skilful means. It is this which makes them pāramīs.

(vi) WHAT IS THEIR CONDITION?

The condition of the pāramīs is, firstly, the great aspiration (*abhinīhāra*). This is the aspiration supported by the eight qualifications (see just below), which occurs thus: "Crossed I would cross, freed I would free, tamed I would tame, calmed I would calm, comforted I would comfort, attained to nibbāna I would lead to nibbāna, purified I would purify, enlightened I would enlighten!" This is the condition for all the pāramīs without exception.

The eight qualifications through which the aspiration succeeds are: the human state, the male sex, the cause, the sight of the Master, the going forth, the achievement of noble qualities, extreme dedication, and strong desire (Bv. IIA,v.59).

(1) The human state (*manussatta*): The aspiration for Buddhahood only succeeds when made by one who has attained to the human state of existence, not when made by one existing as a *nāga*, *supaṇṇa*, etc. Why? Because these other states do not correspond with the state of a Buddha (who always arises in the human state).

(2) The male sex (*liṅgasampatti*): For one who has attained to the human state, the aspiration only succeeds when made by a man, not when made by a woman, eunuch, neuter, or hermaphrodite. Why? For the aforesaid reason (i.e. because the Buddha is always of the male sex), and because there is no fulfilment of the required characteristics (in these other cases). As it is said: "This is impossible, bhikkhus, this cannot come to pass, that a woman might become a perfectly enlightened Buddha" (A.i,28).

(3) The cause (*hetu*): the achievement of the necessary supporting conditions. Even for a man, the aspiration only succeeds for one endowed with the necessary supporting conditions, one who has achieved the requisite causal foundation, not for anyone else.

(4) The sight of the Master (*satthāradassana*): the personal presence of the Master. The aspiration only succeeds when made by one aspiring in the presence of a living Buddha. When made after the Exalted One has passed into parinibbāna—before a shrine, at the foot of the Bodhi-tree, in front of an image, or in the presence of paccekabuddhas or the Buddha's disciples—the aspiration does not succeed. Why? Because the recipient lacks the power (necessary to confirm the aspiration). The aspiration only succeeds when made in the presence of the Buddhas, for they alone possess spiritual power adequate to the loftiness of the aspiration.

(5) The going forth (*pabbajjā*): The aspiration succeeds only when made in the presence of the Exalted Buddha by one who has gone forth (into the homeless state of a monk), either as a bhikkhu or as an ascetic who maintains the doctrine of kamma and the moral efficacy of action; it does not succeed for one living in the household state. Why? Because the household state does not correspond with that of a Buddha (who has himself gone forth). The great bodhisattvas (in their last existence) attain the supreme enlightenment only after they have gone forth into homelessness, not while they are still householders. Therefore, at the time of making the resolution, it is only one who has gone forth, endowed with the appropriate qualities and determination, who can succeed.

(6) The achievement of noble qualities (*guṇasampatti*): the achievement of such noble qualities as the direct knowledges (*abhiññā*), etc. For the aspiration only succeeds when made by one who has gone forth and gained the eight meditative attainments (*samāpatti*) and the five mundane types of direct knowledge;[8] it does not succeed for one devoid of these qualities. Why? Because one devoid of them is incapable of investigating the pāramīs. It is because he possesses the necessary supporting conditions and the direct knowledges that the Great Man, after he has made the aspiration, is able to investigate the pāramīs by himself.

(7) Extreme dedication (*adhikāra*): extreme devotion. The aspiration only succeeds for one endowed with the aforesaid qualities
who at the time has such strong devotion for the Buddhas that he is
prepared to relinquish his very life for them.

(8) Strong desire (*chandatā*): wholesome desire, the wish for
accomplishment. One possessed of the aforesaid qualities must have
strong desire, yearning, and longing to practise the qualities issuing
in Buddhahood. Only then does his aspiration succeed, not other-
wise.

The following similes illustrate the magnitude of the desire required. If he were to hear: "He alone can attain Buddhahood who
can cross a whole world-system filled with water and reach the
further shore by the bare strength of his arms"—he would not deem
that difficult to do, but would be filled with desire for the task and
would not shrink away. If he were to hear: "He alone can attain
Buddhahood who can tread across a whole world-system filled with
flameless, smokeless redhot coals, cross out, and reach the other
side," etc.... If he were to hear: "He alone can attain Buddhahood
who can tread across a whole world-system that has become a solid
mass of sharp-pointed swordstakes, cross out, and reach the other
side," etc.... If he were to hear: "He alone can attain Buddhahood
who can cut through a whole world-system that has become a jun-
gle of thorny creepers covered by a solid thicket of bamboo, cross
out, and reach the other side," etc.... If he were to hear: "Buddhahood can only be attained after being tortured in hell for four
incalculables and a 100,000 aeons"—he would not deem that difficult to do, but would be filled with desire for the task and would
not shrink away. Such is the magnitude of the desire required.

The aspiration, made by one endowed with these eight factors,
is in denotation the act of consciousness (*cittuppāda*) occurring
together with the collection of these eight factors. Its characteristic
is rightly resolving to attain the supreme enlightenment. Its function
is to yearn, "Oh, may I awaken to the supreme perfect enlightenment,
and bring well-being and happiness to all beings!" It is manifest as
the root-cause for the requisites of enlightenment. Its proximate

cause is great compassion, or the achievement of the necessary supporting conditions. Since it has as its object the inconceivable plane of the Buddhas and the welfare of the whole immeasurable world of beings, it should be seen as the loftiest, most sublime and exalted distinction of merit, endowed with immeasurable potency, the root-cause of all the qualities issuing in Buddhahood. Simultaneous with its arising, the Great Man enters upon the practice of the vehicle to great enlightenment (*mahābodhiyānapaṭipatti*). He becomes fixed in his destiny, irreversible, and therefore properly gains the designation "bodhisattva." His mind becomes fully devoted to the supreme enlightenment in its completeness, and his capacity to fulfil the training in the requisites of enlightenment becomes established. For when their aspiration succeeds, the Great Men correctly investigate all the pāramīs with their self-evolved knowledge which prefigures their future attainment of omniscience. Then they undertake their practice, and fulfil them in due order, as was done by the wise Sumedha when he made his great aspiration.

Like the aspiration, great compassion (*mahākaruṇā*) and skilful means (*upāyakosalla*) are also conditions for the pāramīs. Therein, "skilful means" is the wisdom which transforms giving (and the other nine virtues) into requisites of enlightenment. Through their great compassion and skilful means, the Great Men devote themselves to working uninterruptedly for the welfare of others without any concern for their own happiness and without any fear of the extremely difficult course of conduct that great bodhisattvas must follow. And their nature is such that they are able to promote the welfare and happiness of beings even on occasions when they are merely seen, heard of, or recollected, (since even the sight, report, or thought of them) inspires confidence. Through his wisdom the bodhisattva perfects within himself the character of a Buddha, through his compassion the ability to perform the work of a Buddha. Through wisdom he brings himself across (the stream of becoming), through compassion he leads others across. Through wisdom he understands the suffering of others, through compassion he strives to alleviate their suffering. Through wisdom he becomes disenchanted with suffering, through compassion he accepts suffering. Through wisdom he aspires for nibbāna, through compassion he remains in the round of existence. Through compassion he enters saṁsāra, through wisdom he does not delight in it. Through wisdom he destroys all attachments, but because his wisdom is accompanied by compassion he never desists from activity that benefits others. Through compassion he shakes with sympathy for all, but because his compassion is accompanied by wisdom his mind is unattached. Through wisdom he is free from "I-making" and "mine-making," through compassion he is free from lethargy and depression.

So too, through wisdom and compassion respectively, he becomes his own protector and the protector of others, a sage and a hero, one who does not torment himself and one who does not torment others, one who promotes his own welfare and the welfare of others, fearless and a giver of fearlessness, dominated by consideration for the Dhamma and by consideration for the world, grateful for favours done and forward in doing favours for others, devoid of delusion and devoid of craving, accomplished in knowledge and accomplished in conduct, possessed of the powers and possessed of the grounds of self-confidence. Thus wisdom and compassion, as the means for attaining each of the specific fruits of the pāramitās, is the condition for the pāramīs. And the same pair is a condition for the resolution as well.

The four factors—zeal, adroitness, stability, and beneficent conduct—are likewise conditions for the pāramīs. Because they serve as the basis for the arising of Buddhahood, these factors are called "grounds for Buddhahood" (*buddhabhūmiyo*). Herein, "zeal" (*ussāha*) means energy in striving for the requisites of enlightenment. "Adroitness" (*ummaṅga*) is wisdom in applying skilful means to the requisites of enlightenment. "Stability" (*avatthāna*) is determination, an unshakeable determination of the will. "Beneficent conduct" (*hitacariyā*) is the development of loving-kindness and compassion.

Another set of conditions is the six inclinations—the inclinations towards renunciation, solitude, non-greed, non-hatred, non-delusion, and escape. For bodhisattvas, seeing the fault in sense pleasures and in household life, incline to renunciation. Seeing the fault in company, they incline to solitude. Seeing the faults in greed, hatred, and delusion, they incline to non-greed, non-hatred, and non-delusion. Seeing the fault in all the realms of existence, bodhisattvas incline to escape. Therefore these six inclinations of bodhisattvas are conditions for the pāramīs. For the pāramīs do not arise without seeing the danger in greed, etc., and the superiority of non-greed, etc. The inclination to non-greed, etc., is the slanting of the mind towards relinquishing, etc., because of the superiority of non-greed, etc.

So too, for bodhisattvas striving for enlightenment, the inclination towards each of the ten pāramīs is a condition for the practice of each. For bodhisattvas, through their inclination towards giving, see the fault in its opposite, i.e. in stinginess, and therefore fulfil the perfection of giving. Through their inclination towards virtue, they see the fault in moral depravity, and therefore fulfil the perfection of virtue. Through their inclination towards renunciation, they see the fault in sense pleasures and in household life; through their inclination towards knowing things as they really are, they see the faults in ignorance and perplexity; through their inclination towards energy, they see the fault in laziness; through their inclination towards patience, they see the fault in impatience; through their inclination towards truthfulness, they see the fault in deceptive speech; through their inclination towards determination, they see the fault in lack of determination; through their inclination towards loving-kindness, they see the fault in ill-will; and through their inclination towards equanimity, they see the danger in the vicissitudes of the world. Thus they fulfil the perfection of renunciation and the other perfections down to equanimity. In this way, the inclination towards giving and the other nine virtues, by bringing about the achievement of all the pāramīs, serves as their condition.

Reviewing the danger in their opposites and the benefit in their practice is another condition for the pāramīs; e.g. in the case of the perfection of giving, the danger in non-relinquishing and the benefit in relinquishing. This is the method of reviewing:

(1) The *perfection of giving* should be reflected upon thus: "Possessions such as fields, land, bullion, gold, cattle, buffaloes, slaves, children, wives, etc., bring tremendous harm to those who become attached to them. Because they stimulate desire they are wanted by many people; they can be confiscated by kings and thieves; they spark off disputes and create enemies; they are basically insubstantial; to acquire and protect them one has to harass others; when they are destroyed, many kinds of calamities, such as sorrow, etc., follow; and because of attachment to these things, the mind becomes obsessed with the stain of stinginess, and as a result one is reborn in the plane of misery. On the other hand, one act of relinquishing these things is one step to safety. Hence one should relinquish them with diligence."

Further, when a suppliant asks for something, a bodhisattva should reflect: "He is my intimate friend, for he divulges his own secret to me. He is my teacher, for he teaches me: 'When you go you have to abandon all. Going to the world beyond, you cannot even take your own possessions!' He is a companion helping me to remove my belongings from this world which, like a blazing house, is blazing with the fire of death. In removing this he helps me to get rid of the worry it costs me. He is my best friend, for by enabling me to perform this noble act of giving, he helps me to accomplish the most eminent and difficult of all achievements, the attainment of the plane of the Buddhas."

He should further reflect: "He honours me with a lofty task; therefore I should acknowledge that honour faithfully." And: "Since life is bound to end I should give even when not asked, much more when asked." And: "Those with a lofty temperament search for someone to give to, but he has come to me on his own accord because of my merit." And: "Bestowing a gift upon a suppliant will be beneficial to me as well as to him." And: "Just as I would benefit myself, so should I benefit all the world." And: "If there were no suppliants, how would I fulfil the perfection of giving?" And: "Everything I acquire should be obtained only to give to others." And: "When will beggars feel free to take my belongings on their own accord, without asking?" And: "How can I be dear and agreeable to beggars, and how can they be dear and agreeable to me? How can I give and, after giving, be elated, exultant, filled with rapture and joy? And how can beggars be so on my account? How can my inclination to giving be lofty? How can I give to beggars even without being asked, knowing their heart's desire?" And: "Since there are goods, and beggars have come, not to give them something would be a great deception on my part." And: "How can I relinquish my own life and limbs to those who ask for them?"

He should arouse a desire to give things away without concern by reflecting: "Good returns to the one who gives without his concern, just as the boomerang[9] returns to the one who threw it without his concern." If a dear person asks for something, he should arouse joy by reflecting: "One who is dear is asking me for something." If an indifferent person asks for something, he should arouse joy by reflecting: "Surely, if I give him something he will become my friend, since giving to those who ask wins their affection." And if a hostile person asks for something, he should be especially happy, thinking: "My foe is asking me for something; though he is hostile towards me, by means of this gift he will surely become my dear friend." Thus he should give to neutral and hostile people in the same way he gives to dear people, having first aroused loving-kindness and compassion.

If, due to their cumulative force, states of greed should arise for things which can be given away, the bodhisattva-aspirant should reflect: "Well now, good man, when you made the aspiration for full enlightenment, did you not surrender this body as well as the merit gained in relinquishing it for the sake of helping all beings? Attachment to external objects is like the bathing of an elephant; therefore you should not be attached to anything. Suppose there is a great medicine-tree, and someone in need of its roots takes away its roots; someone in need of its shoots, bark, trunk, limbs, heart-wood, branches, foliage, flowers, or fruits takes away its shoots, bark, trunk, etc. The tree would not be assailed by such thoughts as: 'They are taking away my belongings.' In the same way, when

I have undertaken to exert myself for the welfare of all the world, I should not arouse even the subtlest wrong thought over this wretched, ungrateful, impure body, which I have entrusted to the service of others. And besides, what distinction can be made between the internal material elements (of the body) and the external material elements (of the world)? They are both subject to inevitable breaking-up, dispersal, and dissolution. This is only confused prattle, the adherence to this body as 'This is mine, this am I, this is my self.' I should have no more concern over my own hands, feet, eyes, and flesh than over external things. Instead I should arouse the thought to surrender them to others: 'Let those who need them take them away.'"

As he reflects in this way, resolved upon full enlightenment without concern for his body or life, his bodily, vocal, and mental actions will easily become fully purified. When his bodily, vocal, and mental actions, along with his livelihood, become purified, he abides in the practice of the true way, and through his skilful means in regard to gain and loss, he is able to benefit all beings to an even greater extent by relinquishing material gifts and by giving the gift of fearlessness and the gift of the true Dhamma.

This is the method of reflecting on the perfection of giving.

(2) The *perfection of virtue* should be reflected upon as follows: "Even the waters of the Ganges cannot wash away the stain of hatred, yet the water of virtue is able to do so. Even yellow sandalwood cannot cool the fever of lust, yet virtue is able to remove it. Virtue is the unique adornment of the good, surpassing the adornments cherished by ordinary people, such as necklaces, diadems, and earrings. It is a sweet-scented fragrance superior to incense as it pervades all directions and is always in place; a supreme magical spell which wins the homage of deities and of powerful khattiyas, etc., a staircase ascending to the world of the gods, to the heaven of the Four Great Kings,[10] etc., a means for achieving the jhānas and the direct knowledges; a highway leading to the great city of nibbāna; the foundation for the enlightenment of disciples, paccekabuddhas, and perfectly enlightened Buddhas. And as a means

for the fulfilment of all one's wishes and desires, it surpasses the tree of plenty and the wish-fulfilling gem."

Virtue should be reflected upon as the basis for rapture and joy; as granting immunity from fear of self-reproach, the reproach of others, temporal punishment, and an evil destination after death; as praised by the wise; as the root-cause for freedom from remorse; as the basis for security; and as surpassing the achievements of high birth, wealth, sovereignty, long life, beauty, status, kinsmen, and friends. For great rapture and joy arise in the virtuous man when he reflects on his own accomplishment in virtue: "I have done what is wholesome, I have done what is good, I have built myself a shelter from fear." The virtuous man does not blame himself, and other wise men do not blame him, and he does not encounter the dangers of temporal punishment or an evil destination after death. To the contrary, the wise praise the noble character of the virtuous man, and the virtuous man is not subject to the remorse which arises in the immoral man when he thinks: "I have committed evil, wicked, sinful deeds." And virtue is the supreme basis for security, since it is the foundation for diligence, a blessing, and a means for achiev-ing great benefits, such as preventing the loss of wealth, etc.

Accomplishment in virtue surpasses birth in a good family, since a virtuous man of low birth deserves to be worshipped even by great, powerful khattiyas. Virtue surpasses material wealth, for it cannot be confiscated by thieves, follows one to the world beyond, produces great fruit, and acts as the foundation for such qualities as serenity, etc. Because it enables one to achieve supreme sovereignty over one's own mind, virtue surpasses the sovereignty of khattiyas, etc. And because of their virtue, beings attain sovereignty in their respective orders. Virtue is superior even to life, for it is said that a single day in the life of the virtuous is better than a hundred years of life devoid of virtue (Dhp.110); and there being life, the dis-avowal of the training (in the holy life) is called (spiritual) death. Virtue surpasses the achievement of beauty, for it makes one beau-tiful even to one's enemies, and it cannot be vanquished by the adversities of ageing and sickness. As the foundation for distinguished states of happiness, virtue surpasses such distinguished dwellings as palaces, mansions, etc., and such distinguished social positions as that of a king, prince, or general. Because it promotes one's highest welfare and follows one to the world beyond, virtue surpasses kinsmen and friends, even those who are close and affectionate. Again, in accomplishing the difficult task of self-protection, virtue is superior to troops of elephants, horses, chariots, and infantry, as well as to such devices as mantras, spells, and blessings, for it depends on oneself, does not depend on others, and has a great sphere of influence. Hence it is said: "Dhamma protects the one who lives by Dhamma" (Thag.303).

When one reflects in this way upon the numerous noble qualities of virtue, one's unfulfilled achievement of virtue will become fulfilled, and one's unpurified virtue will become purified.

If, due to their cumulative force, states antithetical to virtue such as aversion should arise from time to time, the aspirant should reflect: "Did you not make the resolution to win full enlightenment? One defective in virtue cannot even succeed in mundane affairs, much less in supramundane matters. You should reach the peak of virtue, for virtue is the foundation for supreme enlightenment, the foremost of all achievements. You should always be well behaved, safeguarding your virtue perfectly, more carefully than a hen safeguarding its eggs. Further, by teaching the Dhamma you should help beings to enter and reach maturity in the three vehicles (see pp.1–2). But the word of a morally dubious man is no more reliable than the remedy of a doctor who does not consider what is suitable for his patients. How can I be trustworthy, so that I can help beings to enter and reach maturity in the three vehicles? I must be pure in character and in virtue. How can I acquire the distinguished attainments such as the jhānas, etc., so that I will be capable of helping others and of fulfilling the prefection of wisdom, etc.? The distinguished attainments such as the jhānas, etc., are not possible without purification of virtue. Therefore virtue should be made perfectly pure."

(3) The *perfection of renunciation* should be reflected upon by

first discerning the dangers in household life, according to the text "household life is constricting, a path for the dust of passions," etc. (D.i,63); in sense pleasures, according to the text, "sense pleasures are like a chain of bones," etc. (M.i,364); and in sensual desire, according to the text "suppose a man borrowed a loan and undertook work," etc. (D.i,71). Then, in the opposite way, one should reflect upon the benefits in going forth, according to the text "going forth is like open space," etc. (D.i,63). This is a brief statement. For details one should consult such suttas as "The Great Mass of Suffering" (M.i,83-90) or "The Simile of the Venomous Snakes" (S.iv,172-75).

(4) For the *perfection of wisdom*, the noble qualities of wisdom should be considered, as follows: "Without wisdom, the virtues such as giving do not become purified and cannot perform their respective functions. Just as, without life, the bodily organism loses its luster and cannot perform its proper activities, and as without consciousness the sense faculties cannot exercise their functions in their respective spheres, just so, without wisdom the faculties such as faith, etc., cannot perform their functions. Wisdom is the chief cause for the practice of the other pāramī. For when their wisdom-eyes open up, the great bodhisattvas give even their own limbs and organs without extolling themselves and disparaging others. Like medicine-trees they give devoid of discrimination, filled with joy throughout the three times. By means of wisdom, the act of relinquishing, exercised with skilful means and practised for the welfare of others, attains the status of a pāramī; but giving for one's own benefit is like an investment. Again, without wisdom virtue cannot be severed from the defilements of craving, etc., and therefore cannot even reach purification, much less serve as the foundation for the qualities of an omniscient Buddha. Only the man of wisdom clearly recognizes the dangers in household life, in the strands of sense pleasure, and in saṁsāra, and sees the benefits in going forth, in attaining the jhānas, and in realizing nibbāna; and he alone goes forth into homelessness, develops the jhānic attainments, and, directed towards nibbāna, establishes others therein.

"Energy devoid of wisdom does not accomplish the purpose desired since it is wrongly aroused, and it is better not to arouse energy at all than to arouse it in the wrong way. But when energy is conjoined with wisdom, there is nothing it cannot accomplish if equipped with the proper means. Again, only the man of wisdom can patiently tolerate the wrongs of others, not the dull-witted man. In the man lacking wisdom, the wrongs of others only provoke impatience; but for the wise, they call his patience into play and make it grow even stronger. The wise man, having understood as they really are three noble truths,[11] their causes and opposites, never speaks deceptively to others. So too, having fortified himself with the power of wisdom, the wise man in his fortitude forms an unshakeable determination to undertake all the pāramīs. Only the man of wisdom is skilful in providing for the welfare of all beings, without discriminating between dear people, neutrals, and enemies. And only by means of wisdom can he remain indifferent to the vicissitudes of the world, such as gain and loss, without being affected by them."

In this way one should reflect upon the noble qualities of wisdom, recognizing it to be the cause for the purification of all the pāramīs.

Furthermore, without wisdom there is no achievement of vision, and without the achievement of vision there can be no accomplishment in virtue. One lacking virtue and vision cannot achieve concentration, and without concentration one cannot even secure one's own welfare, much less the lofty goal of providing for the welfare of others. Therefore a bodhisattva, practising for the welfare of others, should admonish himself: "Have you made a thorough effort to purify your wisdom?" For it is by the spiritual power of wisdom that the Great Beings, established in the four foundations, benefit the world with the four bases of beneficence, help beings enter the path to emancipation, and bring their faculties to maturity.[12] Through the power of wisdom, again, they are devoted to the investigation of the aggregates, sense bases, etc., fully comprehend the processes of origination and cessation in accordance with actuality, develop the qualities of giving, etc., to the stages of distinction and penetration, and perfect the training of bodhisattvas. Thus the perfection of wisdom should be reinforced by determining the noble qualities of wisdom with their numerous modes and constituents.

(5) The *perfection of energy* should be reflected upon thus: "Without energy a man cannot even achieve success in worldly works directed to visible ends. But there is nothing the energetic, indefatigable man cannot achieve. One lacking energy cannot undertake to rescue all beings from the great flood of saṁsāra; even if his energy is only moderate he will give up in the middle. But one bristling with energy can achieve perfection in all he undertakes."

The noble qualities of energy should be further reviewed as follows: "One intent on rescuing himself alone from the mire of saṁsāra cannot fulfil his ideal if he relaxes his energy; how much less one who aspires to rescue the entire world." And: "Through the power of energy such wrong thoughts as the following are kept away: 'It is quite right for you to escape from the suffering of saṁsāra by yourself alone; for so long as you are a foolish worldling the host of defilements is as difficult to restrain as a herd of mad elephants, the kamma caused by them is like a murderer with drawn sword, the evil destinations based on these actions stand constantly before you with open doors, and evil friends are always around to enjoin you in those actions and admonish you to practise them.'" And: "If even full enlightenment can be achieved by one's own energy, what can be difficult?"

(6) The *perfection of patience* should be considered next: "Patience is the unimpeded weapon of the good in the development of noble qualities, for it dispels anger, the opposite of all such qualities, without residue. It is the adornment of those capable of vanquishing the foe; the strength of recluses and brahmins; a stream of water extinguishing the fire of anger; the basis for acquiring a good reputation; a mantra for quelling the poisonous speech of evil people; the supreme source of constancy in those established in restraint. Patience is an ocean on account of its depth; a shore bounding the great ocean of hatred; a panel closing off the door to the

plane of misery; a staircase ascending to the worlds of the gods and Brahmās; the ground for the habitation of all noble qualities; the supreme purification of body, speech and mind."

Patience should be further fortified by reflection: "Those who lack patience are afflicted in this world and apply themselves to actions which will lead to their affliction in the life to come." And: "Although this suffering arises through the wrong deeds of others, this body of mine is the field for that suffering, and the action which is its seed was sown by me alone." And: "This suffering will release me from the debt of that kamma." And: "If there were no wrong-doers, how could I accomplish the perfection of patience?" And: "Although he is a wrong-doer now, in the past he was my benefactor." And: "A wrong-doer is also a benefactor, for he is the basis for developing patience." And: "All beings are like my own children. Who becomes angry over the misdeeds of his own children?" And: "He wrongs me because of some residue of anger in myself; this residue I should remove." And: "I am just as much the cause as he for the wrong on account of which this suffering has arisen." And: "All those phenomena by which wrong was done, and those to whom it was done—all those, at this very moment, have ceased. With whom, then, should you now be angry, and by whom should anger be aroused? When all phenomena are non-self, who can do wrong to whom?"

If, due to its cumulative force, anger caused by the wrongs of others should continue to overpower the mind, one should reflect: "Patience is the contributive cause for rendering help to others in return for their wrong." And: "This wrong, by causing me suffering, is a condition for faith, since suffering is said to be the decisive support for faith, and it is also a condition for the perception of discontent with all the world." And: "This is the nature of the sense-faculties—to encounter desirable and undesirable objects. How then is it possible not to encounter undesirable objects?" And: "Under the control of anger, a person becomes mad and distraught, so why retaliate?" And: "All these beings are watched over by the Buddha as if they were his own dear children. Therefore I should not be angry with them." And: "When the wrong-doer is endowed with noble qualities, I should not be angry with him. And when he does not have any noble qualities, then I should regard him with compassion." And: "Because of anger my fame and noble qualities diminish, and to the pleasure of my enemies I become ugly, sleep in discomfort, etc." And: "Anger is the only real enemy, for it is the agent of all harm and the destroyer of all good." And: "When one has patience one has no enemies." And: "Because of his wrong, the wrong-doer will meet suffering in the future, but so long as I remain patient I will not." And: "Enemies are the consequence of my angry thought. When I vanquish anger by patience, my foe, who is the by-product of my anger, will also be vanquished." And: "I should not relinquish the noble quality of patience because of a little anger. Anger is the antithesis and obstruction to all noble qualities, so if I become angry, how can my virtue, etc., reach fulfilment? And when those qualities are absent, how can I devote myself to helping other beings and attain the ultimate goal in accordance with my vows." And: "When there is patience, the mind becomes concentrated, free from external distraction. With the mind concentrated, all formations appear to reflection as impermanent and suffering, all phenomena as non-self, nibbāna as unconditioned, deathless, peaceful, and sublime, and the Buddha-qualities as endowed with inconceivable and immeasurable potency. Then, established in acquiescence in conformity,[13] the groundlessness of all 'I-making' and 'mine-making' becomes evident to reflection thus: 'Mere phenomena alone exist, devoid of self or of anything pertaining to a self. They arise and pass away in accordance with their conditions. They do not come from anywhere, they do not go anywhere, they are not established anywhere. There is no agency in anything whatsoever.' In this way a bodhisattva becomes fixed in destiny, bound for enlightenment, irreversible."

This is the method of reflecting upon the perfection of patience.

(7) The *perfection of truthfulness* should be reviewed thus: "Without truthfulness, virtue, etc., is impossible, and there can be no practice in accordance with one's vows. All evil states converge

upon the transgression of truth. One who is not devoted to truth is unreliable and his word cannot be accepted in the future. On the other hand, one devoted to truth secures the foundation of all noble qualities. With truthfulness as the foundation, he is capable of purifying and fulfilling all the requisites of enlightenment. Not deceived about the true nature of phenomena, he performs the functions of all the requisites of enlightenment and completes the practice of the bodhisattva path."

(8) The *perfection of determination* should be reviewed thus: "Without firmly undertaking the practice of giving (and the other pāramīs), maintaining an unshakeable determination in the encounter with their opposites, and practising them with constancy and vigour, the bases of enlightenment—i.e. the requisites such as giving, etc.—do not arise."

(9) The noble qualities of *loving-kindness* should be reflected upon as follows: "One resolved only upon his own welfare cannot achieve success in this world or a happy rebirth in the life to come without some concern for the welfare of others; how then can one wishing to establish all beings in the attainment of nibbāna succeed without loving-kindness? And if you wish to ultimately lead all beings to the supramundane achievement of nibbāna, you should begin by wishing for their mundane success here and now." And: "I cannot provide for the welfare and happiness of others merely by wishing for it. Let me put forth effort to accomplish it." And: "Now I support them by promoting their welfare and happiness; afterwards they will be my companions in sharing the Dhamma." And: "Without these beings, I could not acquire the requisites of enlightenment. Since they are the cause for the manifestation and perfecting of all the Buddha-qualities, these beings are for me a supreme field of merit, the incomparable basis for planting wholesome roots, the ultimate object of reverence."

Thus one should arouse an especially strong inclination towards promoting the welfare of all beings. And why should loving-kindness be developed towards all beings? Because it is the foundation for compassion. For when one delights in providing for the welfare and happiness of other beings with an unbounded heart, the desire to remove their affliction and suffering becomes powerful and firmly rooted. And compassion is the first of all the qualities issuing in Buddhahood—their footing, foundation, root, head and chief.

(10) The *perfection of equanimity* should be considered thus: "When there is no equanimity, the offensive actions performed by beings cause oscillation in the mind. And when the mind oscillates, it is impossible to practise the requisites of enlightenment." And: "Even though the mind has been softened with the moisture of loving-kindness, without equanimity one cannot purify the requisites of enlightenment and cannot dedicate one's requisites of merit along with their results to furthering the welfare of beings."

Moreover, the undertaking, determination, fulfilment, and completion of all the requisites of enlightenment succeed through the power of equanimity. For without equanimity, the aspirant cannot relinquish something without making false discriminations over gifts and recipients. Without equanimity, he cannot purify his virtue without always thinking about the obstacles to his life and to his vital needs. Equanimity perfects the power of renunciation, for by its means he overcomes discontent and delight. It perfects the functions of all the requisites (by enabling wisdom) to examine them according to their origin. When energy is aroused to excess because it has not been examined with equanimity, it cannot perform its proper function of striving. Forbearance and reflective acquiescence (the modes of patience) are possible only in one possessed of equanimity. Because of this quality, he does not speak deceptively about beings or formations. By looking upon the vicissitudes of worldly events with an equal mind, his determination to fulfil the practices he has undertaken becomes completely unshakeable. And because he is unconcerned over the wrongs done by others, he perfects the abiding in loving-kindness. Thus equanimity is indispensable to the practice of all the other pāramīs.

Such is the reflection on the perfection of equanimity.

Thus reviewing the danger in their opposites and the benefits in their practice is a condition for the pāramīs.

(vii) WHAT IS THEIR DEFILEMENT (*saṅkilesa*)?

In general, being misapprehended by craving, etc., is the defilement of all the pāramīs. Taken separately, discriminating thoughts (*vikappa*) over gifts and recipients are the defilement of the perfection of giving. Discriminating thoughts over beings and times are the defilement of the perfection of virtue. Discriminating thoughts of delight in sense pleasures and existence, and of discontent with their pacification, are the defilement of the perfection of renunciation. Discriminating thoughts of "I" and "mine" are the defilement of the perfection of wisdom; discriminating thoughts leaning to listlessness and restlessness, of the perfection of energy; discriminating thoughts of oneself and others, of the perfection of patience; discriminating thoughts of avowing to have seen what was not seen, etc., of the perfection of truthfulness; discriminating thoughts perceiving flaws in the requisites of enlightenment and virtues in their opposites, of the perfection of determination; discriminating thoughts confusing what is harmful with what is beneficial, of the perfection of loving-kindness; and discriminating thoughts over the desirable and undesirable, of the perfection of equanimity. Thus the defilements should be understood.

(viii) WHAT IS THEIR CLEANSING (*vodāna*)?

Their cleansing is the removal of the taints of craving, etc., and the absence of the aforementioned discriminations. For the pāramīs become pure and luminous when untainted by such defilements as craving, conceit, views, anger, malice, denigration, domineering, envy, stinginess, craftiness, hypocrisy, obstinacy, presumption, vanity, and negligence, and when devoid of the discriminating thoughts over gifts and recipients, etc.

(ix) WHAT ARE THEIR OPPOSITES (*paṭipakkha*)?

In general, all the defilements and all unwholesome qualities are their opposites. Taken separately, stinginess is the opposite of giving, and so on, as mentioned earlier. Further, giving is opposed to greed, hatred, and delusion, since it applies the qualities of non-greed, non-hatred, and non-delusion to gifts, recipients, and the fruits of giving, respectively. Virtue is opposed to greed, hatred, and delusion, since it removes crookedness and corruption in bodily conduct, etc. Renunciation is opposed to these three corruptions since it avoids indulgence in sense pleasures, the affliction of others, and self-mortification. Wisdom opposes them in so far as greed, etc., create blindness, while knowledge restores sight. Energy opposes them by arousing the true way free from both listlessness and restlessness. Patience opposes them by accepting the desirable, the undesirable, and emptiness. Truthfulness is their opposite because it proceeds in accordance with fact whether others render help or inflict harm. Determination is the opposite of these three defilements since, after vanquishing the vicissitudes of the world, it remains unshakeable in fulfilling the requisites of enlightenment in the way they have been undertaken. Loving-kindness is the opposite of greed, hatred, and delusion, through its seclusion from the hindrances. And equanimity is their opposite by dispelling attraction and repulsion towards desirable and undesirable objects, respectively, and by proceeding evenly under varying circumstances.

(x) HOW ARE THEY TO BE PRACTISED?

(1) The *perfection of giving*, firstly, is to be practised by benefiting beings in many ways—by relinquishing one's own happiness, belongings, body, and life to others, by dispelling their fear, and by instructing them in the Dhamma. Herein, giving is threefold by way of the object to be given: the giving of material things (*āmisa-dāna*), the giving of fearlessness (*abhayadāna*), and the giving of the Dhamma (*dhammadāna*). Among these, the object to be given can be twofold: internal and external. The external gift is tenfold: food, drink, garments, vehicles, garlands, scents, unguents, bedding, dwellings, and lamps. These gifts, again, become manifold by analyzing each into its constituents, e.g. food into hard food, soft food, etc. The external gift can also become sixfold when analyzed by way of sense object (*ārammaṇato*): visible forms,

sounds, smells, tastes, tangibles, and non-sensory objects. The sense objects, such as visible forms, become manifold when analyzed into blue, etc. So too, the external gift is manifold by way of the divers valuables and belongings such as gems, gold, silver, pearls, coral, etc.; fields, lands, parks, etc.; slaves, cows, buffaloes, etc.

When the Great Man gives an external object, he gives whatever is needed to whomever stands in need of it; and knowing by himself that someone is in need of something, he gives it even unasked, much more when asked. He gives generously, not ungenerously. He gives sufficiently, not insufficiently, when there is something to be given. He does not give because he expects something in return. And when there is not enough to give sufficiently to all, he distributes evenly whatever can be shared. But he does not give things that issue in affliction to others, such as weapons, poisons, and intoxicants. Nor does he give amusements which are harmful and lead to negligence. And he does not give unsuitable food or drink to a person who is sick, even though he might ask for it, and he does not give what is suitable beyond the proper measure.

Again, when asked, he gives to householders things appropriate for householders, and to monks things appropriate for monks. He gives to his mother and father, kinsmen and relatives, friends and colleagues, children, wife, slaves, and workers, without causing pain to anyone. Having promised an excellent gift, he does not give something mean. He does not give because he desires gain, honour, or fame, or because he expects something in return, or out of expectation of some fruit other than the supreme enlightenment. He does not give detesting the gift or those who ask. He does not give a discarded object as a gift, not even to unrestrained beggars who revile and abuse him. Invariably he gives with care, with a serene mind, full of compassion. He does not give through belief in superstitious omens; but he gives believing in kamma and its fruit. When he gives he does not afflict those who ask by making them do homage to him, etc.; but he gives without afflicting others. He does not give a gift with the intention of deceiving others or with the intention of injuring; he gives only with an undefiled mind. He does not give a gift with harsh words or a frown, but with words of endearment, congenial speech, and a smile on his face. Whenever greed for a particular object becomes excessive, due to its high value and beauty, its antiquity, or personal attachment, the bodhisattva recognizes his greed, quickly dispels it, seeks out some recipients, and gives it away. And if there should be an object of limited value that can be given and a suppliant expecting it, without a second thought he bestirs himself and gives it to him, honouring him as though he were an uncelebrated sage. Asked for his own children, wife, slaves, workers, and servants, the Great Man does not give them while they are as yet unwilling to go, afflicted with grief. But when they are willing and joyful, then he gives them. But if he knows that those who ask for them are demonic beings—ogres, demons, or goblins—or men of cruel disposition, then he does not give them away. So too, he will not give his kingdom to those intent on the harm, suffering, and affliction of the world, but he would give it away to righteous men who protect the world with Dhamma.

This, firstly, is the way to practise the giving of external gifts.

The internal gift should be understood in two ways. How? Just as a man, for the sake of food and clothing, surrenders himself to another and enters into servitude and slavery, in the same way the Great Man, wishing for the supreme welfare and happiness of all beings, desiring to fulfil his own perfection of giving, with a spiritually-oriented mind, for the sake of enlightenment, surrenders himself to another and enters into servitude, placing himself at the disposal of others. Whatever limbs or organs of his might be needed by others—hands, feet, eyes, etc.—he gives them away to those who need them, without trembling and without cowering. He is no more attached to them, and no more shrinks away (from giving them to others), than if they were external objects. Thus the Great Man relinquishes an internal object in two ways: for the enjoyment of others according to their pleasure; or, while fulfilling the wishes of those who ask, for his own self-mastery. In this matter he is completely generous, and thinks: "I will attain enlightenment through non-attachment." Thus the giving of the internal gift should be understood.

Herein, giving an internal gift, he gives only what leads to the welfare of the recipient, and nothing else. The Great Man does not knowingly give his own body, limbs, and organs to Māra or to the malevolent deities in Māra's company, thinking: "Let this not lead to their harm." And likewise, he does not give to those possessed by Māra or his deities, or to madmen. But when asked for these things by others, he gives immediately, because of the rarity of such a request and the difficulty of making such a gift.

The giving of fearlessness is the giving of protection to beings when they have become frightened on account of kings, thieves, fire, water, enemies, lions, tigers, other wild beasts, dragons, ogres, demons, goblins, etc.

The giving of the Dhamma is an unperverted discourse on the Dhamma given with an undefiled mind; that is, methodical instruction conducive to good in the present life, in the life to come, and to ultimate deliverance. By means of such discourses, those who have not entered the Buddha's Dispensation enter it, while those who have entered it reach maturity therein. This is the method: In brief, he gives a talk on giving, on virtue, and on heaven, on the unsatisfactoriness and defilement in sense pleasures, and on the benefit in renouncing them. In detail, to those whose minds are disposed towards the enlightenment of disciples, he gives a discourse establishing and purifying them (in progress towards their goal) by elaborating upon the noble qualities of whichever among the following topics is appropriate: going for refuge, restraint by virtue, guarding the doors of the sense-faculties, moderation in eating, application to wakefulness, the seven good qualities; application to serenity (*samatha*) by practising meditation on one of the thirty-eight objects (of serenity meditation); application to insight (*vipassanā*) by contemplating the objects of insight-interpretation such as the material body; the progressive stages of purification, the apprehension of the course of rightness (*sammattagahaṇa*), the three kinds of clear knowledge (*vijjā*), the six direct knowledges (*abhiññā*), the four discriminations (*paṭisambhidā*), and the enlightenment of a disciple.[14] So too, for beings whose minds are disposed towards the enlightenment of paccekabuddhas and of perfectly enlightened Buddhas, he gives a discourse establishing and purifying them in the two vehicles (leading to these two types of enlightenment) by elaborating upon the greatness of the spiritual power of those Buddhas, and by explaining the specific nature, characteristic, function, etc., of the ten pāramīs in their three stages. Thus the Great Man gives the gift of the Dhamma to beings.

When he gives a material gift, the Great Man gives food thinking: "May I, by this gift, enable beings to achieve long life, beauty, happiness, strength, intelligence, and the supreme fruit of unsullied bliss." He give drink wishing to allay the thirst of sensual defilements; garments to gain the adornments of shame and moral dread and the golden complexion (of a Buddha); vehicles for attaining the modes of psychic potency and the bliss of nibbāna; scents for producing the sweet scent of virtue; garlands and unguents for producing the beauty of the Buddha-qualities; seats for producing the seat on the terrace of enlightenment; bedding for producing the bed of a Tathāgata's rest; dwellings so he might become a refuge for beings; lamps so he might obtain the five-eyes.[15] He gives visible forms for producing the fathom-wide aura (surrounding a Buddha); sounds for producing the Brahmā-like voice (of a Buddha); tastes for endearing himself to all the world; and tangibles for acquiring a Buddha's elegance. He gives medicines so he might later give the ageless and deathless state of nibbāna. He gives slaves the gift of freedom so he might later emancipate beings from the slavery of the defilements. He gives blameless amusements and enjoyments in order to produce delight in the true Dhamma. He gives his own children as a gift in order that he might adopt all beings as his children by granting them a noble birth. He gives his wives as a gift in order that he might become master over the entire world. He gives gifts of gold, gems, pearls, coral, etc., in order to achieve the major marks of physical beauty (characteristic of a Buddha's body),

and gifts of the diverse means of beautification in order to achieve
the minor features of physical beauty.[16] He gives his treasuries as a
gift in order to obtain the treasury of the true Dhamma; the gift of
his kingdom in order to become the king of the Dhamma; the gift
of monasteries, parks, ponds, and groves in order to achieve the
jhānas, etc.; the gift of his feet in order that he might approach the
terrace of enlightenment with feet marked with the auspicious
wheels; the gift of his hands in order that he might give to beings
the rescuing hand of the true Dhamma to help them across the four
floods;[17] the gift of his ears, nose, etc., in order to obtain the spiritual faculties of faith, etc.; the gift of his eyes in order to obtain the
universal eye; the gift of his flesh and blood with the thought: "May
my body be the means of life for all the world! May it bring welfare and happiness to all beings at all times, even on occasions of
merely seeing, hearing, recollecting, or ministering to me!" And he
gives the gift of his head in order to become supreme in all the
world.

Giving thus, the Great Man does not give unwillingly, nor by
afflicting others, nor out of fear, moral shame, or the scolding of
those in need of gifts. When there is something excellent, he does
not give what is mean. He does not give extolling himself and disparaging others. He does not give out of desire for the fruit, nor
with loathing for those who ask, nor with lack of consideration.
Rather, he gives thoroughly, with his own hand, at the proper time,
considerately, without discrimination, filled with joy throughout the
three times.[18] Having given, he does not become remorseful afterwards. He does not become either conceited or obsequious in relation to the recipients, but behaves amiably towards them. Bountiful
and liberal, he gives things together with a bonus (*saparivāra*). For
when he gives food, thinking: "I will give this along with a bonus,"
he gives garments, etc., as well. And when he gives garments, thinking: "I will give this along with a bonus," he gives food, etc., as
well. The same method with gifts of vehicles, etc. And when he
gives a gift of one of the sense objects, such as visible forms, he
gives the other sense objects also as a bonus.

This entire accomplishment in giving he dedicates to the welfare and happiness of the whole world, and to his own unshakeable emancipation through supreme enlightenment. He dedicates it to the attainment of inexhaustible desire (for the good), inexhaustible concentration, ingenuity, knowledge, and emancipation. In practising the perfection of giving the Great Being should apply the perception of impermanence to life and possessions. He should consider them as shared in common with many, and should constantly and continuously arouse great compassion towards beings. Just as, when a house is blazing, the owner removes all his property of essential value and himself as well without leaving anything important behind, so does the Great Man invariably give, without discrimination and without concern.

This is the method of practising the perfection of giving.

(2) Now comes the method of practising the *perfection of virtue*. Since the Great Man desires to adorn beings with the adornment of the virtue of the omniscient, at the beginning he must first purify his own virtue. Herein, virtue is purified in four modes: (1) by the purification of one's inclinations (*ajjhāsayavisuddhi*); (2) by the undertaking of precepts (*samādāna*); (3) by non-transgression (*avītikkamana*); and (4) by making amends for transgressions (*paṭipākatikaraṇa*). For someone who is dominated by personal ideals is naturally disgusted with evil through the purity of his own inclinations and purifies his conduct by arousing his inward sense of shame. Someone else, who is dominated by a consideration for the world, afraid of evil, purifies his conduct by receiving precepts from another person and by arousing his sense of moral dread. Both establish themselves in virtue through non-transgression. But if, due to forgetfulness, they sometimes break a precept, then through their sense of shame and moral dread, respectively, they quickly make amends for it by the proper means of rehabilitation.

Virtue is twofold as avoidance (*vāritta*) and performance (*cāritta*). Herein, this is the method by which *virtue as avoidance* should be practised. A bodhisattva should have such a heart of sympathy for all beings that he does not feel any resentment towards anyone, even in a dream. Because he is dedicated to helping others, he would no more misappropriate the belongings of others than he would take hold of a poisonous watersnake. If he is a monk, he should live remote from unchastity, abstaining from the seven bonds of sexuality (A.iv,54-56), not to speak of adultery. If he is a householder, he should never arouse even an evil thought of lust for the wives of others. When he speaks, his statements should be truthful, beneficial, and endearing, and his talk measured, timely, and concerned with the Dhamma. His mind should always be devoid of covetousness, ill-will, and perverted views. He should possess the knowledge of the ownership of kamma and have settled faith and affection for recluses and brahmins who are faring and practising rightly.

Because he abstains from unwholesome states and from the unwholesome courses of kamma leading to the four planes of misery and the suffering of the round, and because he is established in the wholesome courses of kamma leading to heaven and liberation, through the purity of his end and the purity of his means the Great Man's wishes for the welfare and happiness of beings succeed immediately, exactly in the way they are formed, and his pāramīs reach fulfilment, for such is his nature. Since he desists from injuring others, he gives the gift of fearlessness to all beings. He perfects the meditation on loving-kindness without trouble, and enjoys the eleven benefits of loving-kindness (A.v,342). He is healthy and robust, attains longevity, abundant happiness, and distinguished characteristics, and eradicates the mental impression of hatred.[19] So too, because he desists from taking what is not given, his possessions cannot be confiscated by thieves, etc. He is unsuspicious to others, dear and agreeable, trustworthy, unattached to prosperity and success, inclined to relinquishing, and he eradicates the mental impression of greed.

By desisting from unchastity he becomes unexcitable, peaceful in body and mind, dear and agreeable, unsuspicious to beings. A good report circulates concerning him. He is without lust or attach-

ment to women, is devoted to renunciation, achieves distinguished
characteristics and eradicates the mental impression of greed.

By desisting from false speech his word comes to be authorita-
tive for others. He is regarded as reliable and trustworthy, one whose
statements are always accepted. He is dear and agreeable to deities.
His mouth gives off a sweet fragrance and his bodily and vocal
conduct are protected. He achieves distinguished characteristics and
eradicates the mental impression of defilements.

By desisting from slander he obtains a retinue and a following
that cannot be divided by the attacks of others. He possesses un-
breakable faith in the true Dhamma. He is a firm friend, as exceed-
ingly dear to beings as though they were acquainted with him in
the last existence. And he is devoted to non-defilement.

By desisting from harsh speech he becomes dear and agreeable
to beings, pleasant in character, sweet in speech, held in esteem.
And he develops a voice endowed with eight factors.[20]

By desisting from idle chatter he becomes dear and agreeable to
beings, revered, held in esteem. His statements are accepted and
his talk measured. He acquires great influence and power, and becomes skilful in answering the questions of others with the ingenuity that creates opportunities (to benefit others). And when he reaches
the plane of Buddhahood, he becomes capable of answering the
numerous questions of beings, speaking numerous languages all
with a single reply.

Through his freedom from covetousness he gains what he wishes
and obtains whatever excellent possessions he needs. He is hon-
oured by powerful khattiyas. He can never be vanquished by his
adversaries, is never defective in his faculties, and becomes the
peerless individual.

Through his freedom from ill-will he gains a pleasant appearance. He is esteemed by others, and because he delights in the welfare of beings, he automatically inspires their confidence. He becomes lofty in character, abides in loving-kindness, and acquires
great influence and power.

Through his freedom from wrong view he gains good compan-

ions. Even if he is threatened with a sharp sword, he will not perform an evil deed. Because he holds to the ownership of kamma,
he does not believe in superstitious omens. His faith in the true
Dhamma is established and firmly rooted. He has faith in the
enlightenment of the Tathāgatas, and no more delights in the diversity of outside creeds than a royal swan delights in a dung heap. He
is skilful in fully understanding the three characteristics (of impermanence, suffering, and non-self), and in the end gains the unob-
structed knowledge of omniscience. Until he attains final enlightenment he becomes the foremost in whatever order of beings (he
happens to be reborn in) and acquires the most excellent achievements.

Thus, esteeming virtue as the foundation for all achievements—
as the soil for the origination of all the Buddha-qualities, the beginning, footing, head, and chief of all the qualities issuing in Buddhahood—and recognizing gain, honour, and fame as a foe in the guise
of a friend, a bodhisattva should diligently and thoroughly perfect
his virtue as a hen guards its eggs: through the power of mindfulness and clear comprehension in the control of bodily and vocal
action, in the taming of the sense-faculties, in purification of livelihood, and in the use of the requisites.

This, firstly, is the method of practising virtue as avoidance.

The practice of *virtue as performance* should be understood as
follows: Herein, at the appropriate time, a bodhisattva practises salu-
tation, rising up, respectful greetings, and courteous conduct towards good friends worthy of reverence. At the appropriate time he
renders them service, and he waits upon them when they are sick.
When he receives well-spoken advice he expresses his apprecia-
tion. He praises the noble qualities of the virtuous and patiently
endures the abuse of antagonists. He remembers help rendered to
him by others, rejoices in their merits, dedicates his own merits to
the supreme enlightenment, and always abides diligently in the practice of wholesome states. When he commits a transgression he
acknowledges it as such and confesses it to his co-religionists.
Afterwards he perfectly fulfils the right practice.

He is adroit and nimble in fulfilling his duties towards beings when these are conducive to their good. He serves as their companion. When beings are afflicted with the suffering of disease, etc., he prepares the appropriate remedy. He dispels the sorrow of those afflicted by the loss of wealth, etc. Of a helpful disposition, he restrains with Dhamma those who need to be restrained, rehabilitates them from unwholesome ways, and establishes them in wholesome courses of conduct. He inspires with Dhamma those in need of inspiration. And when he hears about the loftiest, most difficult, inconceivably powerful deeds of the great bodhisattvas of the past, issuing in the ultimate welfare and happiness of beings, by means of which they reached perfect maturity in the requisites of enlightenment, he does not become agitated and alarmed, but reflects: "Those Great Beings were only human beings. But by developing themselves through the orderly fulfilment of the training they attained the loftiest spiritual power and the highest perfection in the requisites of enlightenment. I, too, should practise the same training in virtue, etc. In that way I, too, will gradually fulfil the training and in the end attain the same state." Then, with unflagging energy preceded by this faith, he perfectly fulfils the training in virtue, etc.

Again, he conceals his virtues and reveals his faults. He is few in his wishes, content, fond of solitude, aloof, capable of enduring suffering, and free from anxiety. He is not restless, puffed up, fickle, scurrilous, or scattered in speech, but calm in his faculties and mind. Avoiding such wrong means of livelihood as scheming, etc., he is endowed with proper conduct and a suitable resort (for alms). He sees danger in the slightest faults, and having undertaken the rules of training trains himself in them, energetic and resolute, without regard for body or life. He does not tolerate even the slightest concern for his body or life but abandons and dispels it; how much more then excessive concern? He abandons and dispels all the corruptions such as anger, malice, etc., which are the cause for moral depravity. He does not become complacent over some minor achievement of distinction and does not shrink away, but strives for successively higher achievements. In this way the achievements he gains do not partake of diminution or stagnation.

The Great Man serves as a guide for the blind, explaining to them the right path. To the deaf he gives signals with gestures of his hands, and in that way benefits them with good. So too for the dumb. To cripples he gives a chair, or a vehicle, or some other means of conveyance. He strives that the faithless may gain faith, that the lazy may generate zeal, that those of confused mindfulness may develop mindfulness, that those with wandering minds may become accomplished in concentration, and that the dull-witted may acquire wisdom. He strives to dispel sensual desire, ill-will, sloth-and-torpor, restlessness-and-worry, and perplexity in those obsessed by these hindrances, and to dispel wrong thoughts of sensuality, ill-will, and aggression in those subjugated by these thoughts. Out of gratitude to those who have helped him, he benefits and honours them with a similar or greater benefit in return, congenial in speech and endearing in his words.

He is a companion in misfortune. Understanding the nature and character of beings, he associates with whatever beings need his presence, in whatever way they need it; and he practises together with whatever beings need to practise with him, in whatever way of practice is necessary for them. But he proceeds only by rehabilitating them from the unwholesome and establishing them in the wholesome, not in other ways. For in order to protect the minds of others, bodhisattvas behave only in ways which increase the wholesome. So too, because his inclination is to benefit others, he should never harm them, abuse them, humiliate them, arouse remorse in them, or incite them to act in ways which should be avoided. Nor should he place himself in a higher position than those who are of inferior conduct. He should be neither altogether inaccessible to others, nor too easily accessible, and he should not associate with others at the wrong time.

He associates with beings whom it is proper to associate with at the appropriate time and place. He does not criticize those who are dear to others in front of them, nor praise those who are resented by them. He is not intimate with those who are not trustworthy. He does not refuse a proper invitation, or engage in persuasion, or accept excessively. He encourages those endowed with faith with a discourse on the benefits of faith; and he encourages as well those endowed with virtue, learning, generosity, and wisdom with a discourse on the benefits of those qualities. If the bodhisattva has attained to the direct knowledges, he may inspire a sense of spiritual urgency (*saṁvega*) in the negligent by showing them the fate of those in hell, etc., as is fit. Thereby he establishes the faithless (immoral, ignorant, stingy, and dull-witted) in faith (virtue, learning, generosity, and wisdom). He makes them enter the Buddha's Dispensation and brings to maturity those already endowed with these qualities. In this way, through his virtuous conduct, the Great Man's immeasurable flood of merit and goodness ascends to ever increasing heights.

The detailed explanation of virtue is given in diverse ways in the *Visuddhimagga* (Chapter I), in the passage beginning: "Virtue is the states beginning with volition present in one who abstains from the destruction of life, etc., or in one who fulfils the practice of the duties." All that should be brought in here. Only there is this distinction: in that work the discussion of virtue has come down for beings who seek the enlightenment of disciples; but here, because the discussion is intended for great bodhisattvas, it should be explained making compassion and skilful means the forerunners. Just as the Great Man does not dedicate the merits from his practice of virtue to his own release from affliction in the unfortunate destinations, or to his own achievement of kingship in the fortunate destinations, or to becoming a world-ruling monarch, a god, Sakka, Māra, or Brahmā, so too he does not dedicate it to his own attainment of the threefold knowledge, the six direct knowledges, the four discriminations, the enlightenment of a disciple, or the enlightenment of a paccekabuddha. But rather he dedicates it only for the purpose of becoming an omniscient Buddha in order to enable all beings to acquire the incomparable adornment of virtue.

This is the method of practising the perfection of virtue.

(3) The *perfection of renunciation* is the wholesome act of consciousness which occurs renouncing sense pleasures and existence, preceded by the perception of their unsatisfactoriness and accompanied by compassion and skilful means. The bodhisattva should practise the perfection of renunciation by first recognizing the unsatisfactoriness in sense pleasures, etc., according to the following method: "For one dwelling in a home there is no opportunity to enjoy the happiness of renunciation, etc., because the home life is the dwelling place of all the defilements, because a wife and children impose restrictions (on one's freedom), and because the diverse crafts and occupations such as agriculture and trade lead to numerous entanglements. And sense pleasures, like a drop of honey smeared over the blade of a sword, give limited satisfaction and entail abundant harm. They are fleeting like a show perceived in a flash of lightning; enjoyable only through a perversion of perception like the adornments of a madman; a means of vengeance like a camouflaged pit of excrement; unsatisfying like a thin drink or the water moistening the fingers; afflictive like food which is inwardly rotten; a cause for calamity like a baited hook; the cause of suffering in the three times like a burning fire; a basis for bondage like monkey's glue; a camouflage for destruction like a murderer's cloak; a place of danger like a dwelling in an enemy village; food for the Māra of the defilements like the supporter of one's foes; subject to suffering through change like the enjoyment of a festival; inwardly burning like the fire in the hollow of a tree; fraught with danger like a ball of honey suspended from the bulrushes in an old pit; intensifying thirst like a drink of salt water; resorted to by the vulgar like liquor and wine; and giving little satisfaction like a chain of bones."

Having recognized the unsatisfactoriness in sense pleasures in accordance with this method, he should then, by the reverse method, comtemplate the benefits in renunciation, with a mind slanting, sloping, and inclining towards the happiness of renunciation, solitude, and peace.

Since renunciation is rooted in the going forth (i.e. into the homeless life of a monk), the going forth should be undertaken. If the Great Being is living at a time when no Buddha has arisen in the world, he should go forth under ascetics or wanderers who maintain the doctrine of kamma and the moral efficacy of action. But when the perfectly enlightened Buddhas appear in the world, he should go forth only in their Dispensation. Having gone forth, he should establish himself in virtue, as described above, and in order to cleanse his virtue, should undertake the ascetic practices. For Great Men who undertake the ascetic practices and maintain them properly become few in their wishes and content. The stains of their defilements get washed off in the waters of such noble qualities as effacement, solitude, aloofness from society, the arousal of energy, and ease of maintenance, and all their conduct becomes purified through their blameless rules, observances, and noble qualities. Established in three of the ancient traditions of the ariyans,[21] they are able to achieve the fourth of the ariyan traditions, i.e. delight in meditation, entering and abiding in jhāna, both access and absorption, through whichever among the forty subjects of meditation are appropriate. Thus they completely fulfil the perfection of renunciation.

At this point it would be proper to explain in detail the thirteen ascetic practices and the forty meditation subjects for the development of concentration—i.e. the ten *kasiṇa*-devices, the ten impurities, the ten recollections, the four Brahmavihāras, the four immaterial states, the one perception, and the one analysis. But since all these are explained in complete detail in the *Visuddhimagga*, it should be understood in the way stated there. Only there is this distinction: in that work the subject is explained for beings who seek the enlightenment of disciples. But here, because it is intended for great bodhisattvas, it should be explained making compassion and skilful means the forerunners.

This is the method of practising the perfection of renunciation.

(4) Just as light cannot co-exist with darkness, wisdom cannot co-exist with delusion. Therefore a bodhisattva wishing to accom-

plish the *perfection of wisdom* should avoid the causes of delusion. These are the causes of delusion: discontent, languor, drowsiness, lethargy, delight in company, attachment to sleep, irresoluteness, lack of enthusiasm for knowledge, false over-estimation of oneself, non-interrogation, not maintaining one's body properly, lack of mental concentration, association with dull-witted people, not ministering to those possessed of wisdom, self-contempt, false discrimination, adherence to perverted views, athleticism, lack of a sense of spiritual urgency, and the five hindrances; or, in brief, any states which, when indulged in, prevent the unarisen wisdom from arising and cause the arisen wisdom to diminish. Avoiding these causes of confusion, one should apply effort to learning as well as to the jhānas, etc.

This is an analysis of the sphere of learning: the five aggregates, the twelve sense bases, the eighteen elements, the four truths, the twenty-two faculties, the twelve factors of dependent origination, the foundations of mindfulness, etc., the various classifications of phenomena such as the wholesome, etc., as well as any blameless secular fields of knowledge which may be suitable for promoting the welfare and happiness of beings, particularly grammar. Thus, with wisdom, mindfulness, and energy preceded by skilful means, a bodhisattva should first thoroughly immerse himself in this entire sphere of learning—through study, listening, memorization, learning, and interrogation; then he should establish others in learning. In this way the wisdom born of learning (*sutamayī paññā*) can be developed. So too, out of his wish for the welfare of others, the bodhisattva should develop the wisdom of ingenuity in creating opportunities to fulfil his various duties to his fellow beings and the skilful means in understanding their happiness and misery.

Then he should develop wisdom born of reflection (*cintāmayī paññā*) by first reflecting upon the specific nature of the phenomena such as the aggregates, and then arousing reflective acquiescence in them. Next, he should perfect the preliminary portion of the wisdom born of meditation (*pubbabhāgabhāvanāpaññā*) by developing the mundane kinds of full understanding through the discernment of the specific and general characteristics of the aggregates, etc.[22] To do so, he should fully understand all internal and external phenomena without exception as follows: "This is mere mentality-materiality (*nāmarūpamatta*), which arises and ceases according to conditions. There is here no agent or actor. It is impermanent in the sense of not being after having been; suffering in the sense of oppression by rise and fall; and non-self in the sense of being unsusceptible to the exercise of mastery." Comprehending them in this way, he abandons attachment to them, and helps others to do so as well. Entirely out of compassion, he continues to help his fellow beings enter and reach maturity in the three vehicles, assists them to achieve mastery over the jhānas, deliverances, concentrations, attainments, and mundane direct knowledges, and does not desist until he reaches the very peak of wisdom and all the Buddha-qualities come within his grasp.

The wisdom born of meditation may be divided into two groups. The first comprises the mundane direct knowledges, together with their accessories; namely, the knowledge of the modes of psychic power, the knowledge of the divine ear-element, the knowledge of penetrating other minds, the knowledge of recollecting past lives, the knowledge of the divine eye, the knowledge of kammic retribution, and the knowledge of the future.[23] The second comprises the five purifications—purification of view, purification by overcoming doubt, purification by knowledge and vision of what is and what is not the path, purification by knowledge and vision of the way, and purification by knowledge and vision. The first four of these are mundane, the last is supramundane. After acquiring through study and interrogation a knowledge of the phenomena such as the aggregates, etc., constituting the soil of wisdom, he should establish himself in the two purifications constituting its roots, purification of virtue and purification of mind, and then accomplish the five purifications just mentioned which constitute the trunk of wisdom. Since the method for accomplishing these, along with the analysis of their objective sphere, is explained in complete detail in the *Visuddhimagga*, it should be understood in the way given

there.[24] Only in that work the explanation of wisdom has come
down for beings seeking the enlightenment of disciples. But here,
because it is intended for the great bodhisattvas, it should be explained making compassion and skilful means the forerunners. One
further distinction must also be made: here insight (*vipassanā*)
should be developed only as far as purification by knowledge and
vision of the way, without attaining purification by knowledge and
vision.[25]

*(From this point on the remaining pāramīs are treated piece-
meal and synoptically rather than in systematic detail like the first
four.)*

A Great Being who has formed his aspiration for supreme
enlightenment should, for the sake of fulfilling his pāramīs, always
be devoted to what is proper and intent upon service. Thus he should
be zealous in providing for the welfare of beings, and from time to
time, day by day, should reflect: "Have I accumulated any requisites of merit and of knowledge today? What have I done for the
welfare of others?" In order to help all beings he should surrender
some possession of his with a mind unconcerned with body or life.
Whatever action he does, bodily or vocal, all should be done with a
mind slanting towards full enlightenment; all should be dedicated
to enlightenment. He should turn his mind away from sense pleasures, whether superior or inferior, and should apply skilful means
to the fulfilment of his various duties.

He should work energetically for the welfare of beings, be capable of enduring everything whether desirable or undesirable, and
should speak without deception.[26] He should suffuse all beings with
universal loving-kindness and compassion. Whatever causes suffering for beings, all that he should be ready to take upon himself;
and he should rejoice in the merits of all beings. He should fre-
quently reflect upon the greatness of the Buddhas and the greatness
of their spiritual power. Whatever action he does by body or speech,
all should be preceded with a mind slanting towards full enlightenment. In this way, the Great Being, the bodhisattva, devoted to

what is proper, endowed with strength, firm in striving, day by day accumulates immeasurable requisites of merit and of knowledge through the practice of the pāramīs.

Further, having relinquished his own body and life for the use and protection of beings, the bodhisattva should seek out and apply the antidotes to the various kinds of suffering to which beings are exposed—hunger, thirst, cold, heat, wind, sun, etc. And whatever happiness he himself gains by alleviating these kinds of suffering, and the happiness he gains when his own bodily and mental afflictions subside in delightful parks, gardens, mansions, pools, and forest abodes, and the happiness of the blissful jhānic attainments he hears are experienced by the Buddhas, their enlightened disciples, paccekabuddhas, and great bodhisattvas, established in the practice of renunciation—all that he seeks to procure universally for all beings.

This, firstly, is the method for a bodhisattva not yet established on the plane of concentration. One established on the plane of concentration bestows upon beings the rapture, tranquillity, happiness, concentration, and true knowledge produced in the achievements of distinction as they are experienced by himself. He procures them and dedicates them to all. Such a bodhisattva should contemplate the whole world of sentient beings immersed in the great suffering of saṁsāra and in the sufferings of the defilements and kamma-formations at its base. He should see the beings in hell experiencing violent, racking, agonizing pains uninterruptedly over long periods, produced as they are cut up, dismembered, split, pulverized, and roasted in scorching fires; the great suffering of the animals due to their mutual hostility, as they afflict, harass, and kill one another, or fall into captivity at the hands of others; and the suffering of the various classes of ghosts, going about with their bodies aflame, consumed and withered by hunger, thirst, wind, and sun, weeping and wailing as their food turns into vomit and spittle. He should contemplate as well the suffering experienced by human beings, which is often indistinguishable from the suffering in the plane of misery: the misery and ruin they encounter in their search (for the means of sustenance and enjoyment); the various punishments they may meet, such as the cutting off of their hands, etc.; ugliness, deformity, and poverty; affliction by hunger and thirst; being vanquished by the more powerful, pressed into the service of others, and made dependent upon others; and when they pass away, falling over into the hells, the realm of ghosts, and the animal kingdom. He should see the gods of the sense-sphere being consumed by the fevers of lust as they enjoy their sense objects with scattered minds; living with their fever (of passions) unextinguished like a mass of fire stoked up with blasts of wind and fed with a stock of dry wood; without peace, dejected, and dependent on others. And he should see the gods of the fine-material and immaterial spheres, after so long a life-span, in the end succumb to the law of impermanence, plunging from their heights back down into the round of birth, ageing, and death, like birds swooping swiftly down from the heights of the sky or like arrows shot by a strong archer descending in the distance. And having seen all this, he should arouse a sense of spiritual urgency and suffuse all beings universally with lovingkindness and compassion. Accumulating the requisites of enlightenment in this way by body, speech, and mind without interruption, he should fulfil the perfection of energy, arousing zeal while working thoroughly and perseveringly and acting without cowering, in order that all the pāramīs may reach fulfilment.

While striving for the state of Buddhahood—the store and repository of inconceivable, immeasurable, vast, lofty, stainless, incomparable, undefiled qualities—he should encourage the arising of energy; for such energy is endowed with inconceivable spiritual power, which common people cannot even hear about, much less practise. It is entirely through the spiritual power of energy that the practice of all the requisites of enlightenment succeeds—the threefold arising of the great aspiration, the four grounds for Buddhahood, the four bases of beneficence, the single flavour of compassion, the reflective acquiescence which is the specific condition for the realization of the Buddha-qualities, being untainted amidst all things, the perception of all beings as his own dear chil-

dren, not being fatigued by all the sufferings of saṁsāra, the relinquishing of everything that may be given away, delight in so giving, the determination upon the higher virtue, etc., unshakeableness
therein, rapture and exultation in wholesome actions, the inclination towards seclusion, application to the jhānas, being insatiable
in blameless states, teaching the Dhamma to others as he has learned
it out of the wish for their welfare, firm initiative in setting beings
upon the true path, sagacity and heroism, being imperturbable in
face of the abusive speech and wrongs of others, the determination
upon truth, mastery over the meditative attainments, the attainment
of power through the direct knowledges, the comprehension of the
three characteristics, the accumulation of the requisites for the
supramundane path by practising meditation in the foundations of
mindfulness, etc., and the descent on to the nine supramundane
states.[27] Thus from the time of forming the aspiration until the great
enlightenment, a bodhisattva should perfect his energy thoroughly
and uninterruptedly, without surrendering, so that it might issue in
higher and higher states of distinction. And when this energy succeeds, all the requisites of enlightenment—patience, truthfulness,
determination, etc., as well as giving, virtue, etc.—will succeed;
for all these occur in dependence on energy.

The practice of patience and the rest should be understood in
accordance with the same method.

Thus through giving, relinquishing his own happiness and belongings to others, he practises the benefiting of others in many
ways; through virtue, the protection of their lives, property, and
wives, the non-breach of his word, endearing and beneficial speech,
non-injury, etc.; through renunciation, many kinds of beneficial
conduct such as giving the gift of the Dhamma in return for their
material gifts; through wisdom, skilful means in providing for their
welfare; through energy, the arousing of zeal in his work without
slacking off; through patience, the enduring of the wrongs of
others; through truthfulness, not breaking his pledge to help others
without deception; through determination, remaining unshakeable
in rendering them help even when encountering difficulties; through

loving-kindness, concern for their welfare and happiness; and through equanimity, remaining imperturbable whether others render help or inflict harm.

This is the practice which the great bodhisattva, compassionate for all beings, undertakes for the sake of incalculable beings, by means of which he accumulates immeasurable requisites of merit and knowledge not shared by worldlings. Their condition has been stated. They should be accomplished thoroughly.

(xi) HOW ARE THEY ANALYZED (*ko vibhāgo*)?

They are analyzed into thirty pāramīs: ten (basic) pāramīs, ten intermediate pāramīs (*upapāramī*), and ten ultimate pāramīs (*paramatthapāramī*).

Herein, some teachers say that the ten basic pāramīs are the intermingled bright and dark qualities practised by a bodhisattva who has just formed his aspiration, whose end is the welfare of others, and whose means are directed towards working for this end; the intermediate pāramīs are the bright qualities untainted by any darkness; and the ultimate pāramīs are the qualities which are neither dark nor bright.

Others say that the basic pāramīs are being filled at the commencement (of his career); the intermediate pāramīs are filled on the plane of bodhisattvahood: and the ultimate pāramīs reach perfect fulfilment in all modes on the plane of Buddhahood. Or alternatively, the basic pāramīs involve working for the welfare of others on the plane of bodhisattvahood; the intermediate pāramīs, working for one's own welfare; and the ultimate pāramīs, the fulfilment of the welfare of both oneself and others with the achievement of the Tathāgata's powers and grounds of self-confidence on the plane of Buddhahood. Thus they analyze the pāramīs according to the beginning, middle, and consummation (of the bodhisattva's career) by way of the resolution (to fulfil them), the undertaking (of their practice), and their completion, respectively.

The basic perfection of giving (*dānapāramī*) is the relinquishing of one's children, wives, and belongings such as wealth; the intermediate perfection of giving (*dāna-upapāramī*), the relinquishing of one's own limbs; and the ultimate perfection of giving (*dānaparamatthapāramī*), the relinquishing of one's own life. The three stages in the perfection of virtue should be understood as the non-transgression (of moral conduct) on account of the three—children and wife, limbs, and life; the three stages in the perfection of renunciation, as the renunciation of those three bases after cutting off attachment to them; the three stages in the perfection of wisdom, as the discrimination between what is beneficial and harmful to beings, after rooting out craving for one's belongings, limbs, and life; the three stages in the perfection of energy, as striving for the relinquishing of the aforementioned things; the three stages in the perfection of patience, as the endurance of obstacles to one's belongings, limbs, and life; the three stages in the perfection of truthfulness, as the non-abandoning of truthfulness on account of one's belongings, limbs, and life; the three stages in the perfection of determination, as unshakeable determination despite the destruction of one's belongings, limbs, and life, bearing in mind that the pāramīs ultimately succeed through unflinching determination; the three stages in the perfection of loving-kindness, as maintaining loving-kindness towards beings who destroy one's belongings, etc.; and the three stages in the perfection of equanimity, as maintaining an attitude of impartial neutrality towards beings and formations whether they are helpful or harmful in regard to the aforementioned three bases (i.e. belongings, limbs, and life).

In this way the analysis of the pāramīs should be understood.

(xii) HOW ARE THEY SYNTHESIZED (*ko saṅgaho*)?

Just as the ten pāramīs become thirtyfold through analysis, so they become sixfold through their specific nature: as giving, virtue, patience, energy, meditation, and wisdom.[28]

When this set is considered, the perfection of renunciation, as the going forth into homelessness, is included in the perfection of virtue; as seclusion from the hindrances, in the perfection of meditation; and as a generally wholesome quality, in all six pāramīs.

One part of the perfection of truthfulness, i.e. its aspect of truthful speech or abstinence from falsehood, is included in the perfection of virtue, and one part, i.e. its aspect of truthful knowledge, in the perfection of wisdom. The perfection of loving-kindness is included in the perfection of meditation, and the perfection of equanimity in the perfections of meditation and wisdom. The perfection of determination is included in all.

These six pāramīs fall into at least fifteen pairs (*yugala*) of complementary qualities which perfect fifteen other pairs of qualities. How?

(1) The pair—giving and virtue—perfects the pair of doing what is beneficial for others and abstaining from what is harmful to them.

(2) The pair—giving and patience—perfects the pair of non-greed and non-hatred.

(3) The pair—giving and energy—perfects the pair of generosity and learning.

(4) The pair—giving and meditation—perfects the abandoning of sensual desire and hatred;

(5) the pair giving and wisdom, the noble vehicle and burden;

(6) the dyad of virtue and patience, the purification of means and the purification of the end;

(7) the dyad of virtue and energy, the dyad of meditative development (i.e. serenity and insight);

(8) the dyad of virtue and meditation, the abandoning of moral depravity and of mental obsession;

(9) the dyad of virtue and wisdom, the dyad of giving;[29]

(10) the dyad of patience and energy, the dyad of acceptance and fervour;

(11) the dyad of patience and meditation, the abandoning of opposing and favouring;

(12) the dyad of patience and wisdom, the acceptance and penetration of emptiness;

(13)   the dyad of energy and meditation, the dyad of exertion and non-distraction;

(14)   the dyad of energy and wisdom, the dyad of refuges;

(15)   and the dyad of meditation and wisdom perfects the dyad of vehicles (i.e. the vehicles of serenity and insight).

The triad of giving, virtue, and patience perfects the abandoning of greed, hatred, and delusion. The triad of giving, virtue, and energy perfects the giving of wealth, life, and bodily vitality. The triad of giving, virtue, and meditation perfects the three bases of meritorious deeds. The triad of giving, virtue, and wisdom perfects the triad of giving material gifts, fearlessness, and the Dhamma. In the same way, the other triads and tetrads may be applied to each other as is appropriate in each case.

These six pāramīs are also included in the four foundations (*cattāri adhiṭṭhānāni*), which provide a synthesis of all the pāramīs.[30] What are they? The foundation of truth, the foundation of relinquishment, the foundation of peace, and the foundation of wisdom. Therein, taking them first without distinction: after making his aspiration for the supramundane qualities, the Great Being, filled with compassion for all beings, establishes the foundation of truth by acquiring all the pāramīs in conformity with his vow; the foundation of relinquishment by relinquishing their opposites; the foundation of peace by pacifying their opposites with all the qualities of the pāramīs; and the foundation of wisdom by skilful means in promoting the welfare of others through those same qualities.

Taken separately, *giving* is a proximate cause for the four foundations of wholesome qualities as follows: (1) (for the foundation of truth) since one vows to give to those who ask without deceiving them, gives without violating one's vows, and rejoices without deceiving them about the gift; (2) (for the foundation of relinquishment) through the relinquishing of the opposite qualities such as stinginess, etc.; (3) (for the foundation of peace) through the pacification of greed, hatred, delusion, and fear, in regard to the objects to be given, the recipients, the act of giving, and the loss of the objects to be given, respectively; (4) (and for the foundation of wisdom) through giving according to deserts, at the proper time, in the appropriate manner, and through the pre-eminence of wisdom. *Virtue* is a proximate cause for the four foundations thus: (1) through non-transgression of the restraint undertaken; (2) through the relinquishing of moral depravity; (3) through the pacification of misconduct; and (4) through the pre-eminence of wisdom. *Patience* is a proximate cause for the four foundations thus: (1) through patient acceptance in accordance with one's vow; (2) through the relinquishing of discrimination against others on account of their wrongs; (3) through the pacification of the obsession of anger; and (4) through the pre-eminence of wisdom.

Energy is a proximate cause for the four foundations: (1) through working for the welfare of others in accordance with one's vows; (2) through the relinquishing of dejection; (3) through the pacification of unwholesome qualities; and (4) through the pre-eminence of wisdom. *Meditation* is a proximate cause for the four foundations: (1) through concern for the welfare of the world in accordance with one's vow; (2) through the relinquishing of the hindrances; (3) through the pacification of the mind; and (4) through the pre-eminence of wisdom. And *wisdom* is a proximate cause for the four foundations: (1) through skilful means in promoting the welfare of others in accordance with one's vow; (2) through the relinquishing of unskilful activity; (3) through the pacification of the fevers springing from delusion; and (4) through the attainment of omniscience.

The foundation of truth is practised by acting in accordance with one's vow and understanding; the foundation of relinquishment by relinquishing (outer) objects of sense enjoyment and the (inner) defilement of sensuality; the foundation of peace by the pacification of hatred and suffering; and the foundation of wisdom by understanding and penetration. The foundation of truth is embraced by the threefold truth and opposed to the three corruptions (of greed, hatred and delusion). The foundation of relinquishing is embraced by the threefold relinquishment and opposed to the three corruptions. The foundation of peace is embraced by the threefold pacification and opposed to the three corruptions. And the foundation of wisdom is embraced by the threefold knowledge and opposed to the three corruptions.

The foundation of truth embraces the foundations of relinquishment, peace, and wisdom through non-deceptiveness and through acting in accordance with one's vow. The foundation of relinquishment embraces the foundations of truth, peace, and wisdom through the relinquishing of their opposites and as the fruit of relinquishing everything. The foundation of peace embraces the foundations of truth, relinquishment, and wisdom through the pacification of the fever of defilement and the fever of kamma. And the foundation of wisdom embraces the foundations of truth, relinquishment, and peace, since they are all preceded and accompanied by knowledge. Thus all the pāramīs are grounded in truth, clarified by relinquishment, intensified by peace, and purified by wisdom. For truth is the cause for their genesis, relinquishment the cause for their acquisition, peace the cause for their growth, and wisdom the cause for their purification.

In the beginning (of the bodhisattva's career) truth is the foundation, since his vow is made in accordance with truth. In the middle, relinquishment is the foundation, since after forming his aspiration the bodhisattva relinquishes himself for the welfare of others. In the end, peace is the foundation, since the consummation (of the career) is the attainment of perfect peace. And in every phase—the beginning, the middle, and the end—wisdom is the foundation, since the entire career originates when wisdom is present, does not exist when it is absent, and because the nature (of wisdom) accords with the vow.

Thus it should be understood how the aggregation of the pāramīs is included in the four foundations, which are adorned with numerous noble qualities. And just as the pāramīs are all included in the four foundations, they are also included in wisdom and compassion. For all the requisites of enlightenment can be included in wisdom and compassion, and the noble qualities such as giving (and the other pāramīs), accompanied by wisdom and compassion, are the requisites for the great enlightenment culminating in the perfection of Buddhahood.

(xiii) BY WHAT MEANS ARE THEY ACCOMPLISHED?

The means by which the pāramīs are accomplished is the four-factored method: (1) the accumulation without omission of all the requisites of merit, etc., for the sake of supreme enlightenment, by performing them without deficiency; (2) performing them thoroughly with respect and high esteem; (3) performing them perseveringly without interruption; and (4) enduring effort over a long period without coming to a halt half-way. We will explain the length of time later.

For the sake of the supreme enlightenment, the Great Being, striving for enlightenment, should first of all surrender himself to the Buddhas thus: "I offer myself up to the Buddhas." And whenever he obtains any possession, he should first of all resolve upon it as a potential gift: "Whatever requisite of life comes my way, that I will give to those who need it, and I myself will only use what remains over from this gift."

When he has made a mental determination to completely relinquish whatever possessions come his way, whether animate or inanimate, there are four shackles to giving (which he must overcome), namely: not being accustomed to giving in the past, the inferiority of the object to be given, the excellence and beauty of the object, and worry over the loss of the object.

(1) When the bodhisattva possesses objects that can be given and suppliants are present, but his mind does not leap up at the thought of giving and he does not want to give, he should conclude: "Surely, I have not been accustomed to giving in the past; therefore a desire to give does not arise now in my mind. So that my mind will delight in giving in the future, I will give a gift. With an eye for the future let me now relinquish what I have to those in need." Thus he gives a gift—generous, open-handed, delighting in relinquishing, one who gives when asked, delighting in giving and

in sharing. In this way the Great Being destroys, shatters, and eradicates the first shackle to giving.

(2) Again, when the object to be given is inferior or defective, the Great Being reflects: "Because I was not inclined to giving in the past, at present my requisites are defective. Therefore, though it pains me, let me give whatever I have as a gift even if the object is low and inferior. In that way I will, in the future, reach the peak in the perfection of giving." Thus he gives whatever kind of gift he can—generous, open-handed, delighting in relinquishing, one who gives when asked, delighting in giving and in sharing. In this way the Great Being destroys, shatters, and eradicates the second shackle to giving.

(3) When a reluctance to give arises due to the excellence or beauty of the object to be given, the Great Being admonishes himself: "Good man, haven't you made the aspiration for the supreme enlightenment, the loftiest and most superior of all states? Well then, for the sake of enlightenment, it is proper for you to give excellent and beautiful objects as gifts." Thus he gives what is excellent and beautiful—generous, open-handed, delighting in relinquishing, one who gives when asked, delighting in giving and in sharing. In this way the Great Man destroys, shatters, and eradicates the third shackle to giving.

(4) When the Great Being is giving a gift, and he sees the loss of the object being given, he reflects thus: "This is the nature of material possessions, that they are subject to loss and to passing away. Moreover, it is because I did not give such gifts in the past that my possessions are now depleted. Let me then give whatever I have as a gift, whether it be limited or abundant. In that way in the future I shall reach the peak in the perfection of giving." Thus he gives whatever he has as a gift—generous, open-handed, delighting in relinquishing, one who gives when asked, delighting in giving and in sharing. In this way the Great Being destroys, shatters, and eradicates the fourth shackle to giving.

Reflecting upon them thus in whatever way is appropriate is the means for dispelling the harmful shackles to the perfection of giving. The same method used for the perfection of giving also applies to the perfection of virtue and the other perfections.

Further, self-surrender to the Buddhas is also a means for the complete accomplishment of the pāramīs. For when the Great Man, straining and striving for the fulfilment of the requisites of enlightenment, encounters troubles difficult to endure, depriving him of happiness and his means of support, or when he encounters injuries imposed by beings and formations—difficult to overcome, violent, sapping the vitality—then, since he has surrendered himself to the Buddhas, he reflects: "I have relinquished my very self to the Buddhas. Whatever comes, let it come." For this reason he does not waver, does not quake, does not undergo the least vacillation, but remains absolutely unshaken in his determination to undertake the good.

In brief, the destruction of self-love and the development of love for others are the means for the accomplishing of the pāramīs. For by fully understanding all things in accordance with their nature, the Great Being who has formed the resolution to attain the supreme enlightenment remains untainted by them, and his self-love thereby becomes eliminated and exhausted. Then, since through the repeated practice of great compassion he has come to regard all beings as his dear children, his loving-kindness, compassion, and affection for them increase. In conformity with this stage the Great Man, having expelled the defilements such as stinginess, etc., that are opposed to the requisites of enlightenment, and having dispelled greed, hatred, and delusion in regard to himself and others, further causes people to enter and reach maturity in the three vehicles by benefiting them to the utmost with the four bases of beneficence which accompany the four foundations, namely: giving, loving speech, beneficent conduct, and equality of treatment.

For the great compassion and the great wisdom of the Great Beings are adorned by giving. Their giving is adorned and accompanied by loving speech, loving speech by beneficent conduct, and beneficent conduct by equality of treatment. When the bodhisattvas are practising the requisites of enlightenment, they treat all beings without exception as equal to themselves and perfect their sense of equality by remaining the same under all circumstances, pleasant or painful. And when they become Buddhas, their ability to train people is perfected by benefiting them to the utmost with these same four bases of beneficence brought to fulfilment by the four foundations. For the perfectly enlightened Buddhas, the base of giving is brought to fulfilment by the foundation of relinquishment, the base of loving speech by the foundation of truth, the base of beneficent conduct by the foundation of wisdom, and the base of equal treatment by the foundation of peace. For in regard to parinibbāna, all the disciples and paccekabuddhas are completely equal to the Tathāgatas; they are identical, without any distinction. Thus it is said: "There is no diversity among them in regard to emancipation."

> He is truthful, generous, and peaceful,
> Endowed with wisdom and sympathy,
> Complete in all the requisites:
> What good can he not achieve?

> He is the great compassionate Teacher,
> Equanimous yet seeking the welfare of all,
> Free from concern on all occasions:
> Oh, how wonderful is the Conqueror!

> Dispassionate towards all things of the world,
> And towards all beings of equal mind,
> Still he abides devoted to their welfare:
> Oh, how wonderful is the Conqueror!

> Always engaged in work promoting
> The welfare and happiness of all beings,
> He never ceases on account of the trouble:
> Oh, how wonderful is the Conqueror!

(xiv) HOW MUCH TIME IS REQUIRED TO ACCOMPLISH THEM?

As a minimum, four incalculables (*asaṅkheyya*) and a hundred thousand great aeons (*mahākappa*); as a middle figure, eight incalculables and a hundred thousand great aeons; and as a maximum, sixteen incalculables and a hundred thousand great aeons.[31] This threefold division obtains by way of those in whom wisdom is predominant, those in whom faith is predominant, and those in whom energy is predominant, respectively. For those in whom wisdom is predominant, faith is weakest and wisdom keenest; for those in whom faith is predominant, wisdom is middling (and energy weakest); and for those in whom energy is predominant, wisdom is weakest (and faith middling). But supreme enlightenment must be achieved by the power of wisdom; so it is said in the commentary.

But others say that the classification of the time required for bodhisattvas obtains by way of the keen, middling, and tender quality of their energy. Still others say that without distinction the three divisions of time correspond to the time required for their requisites of enlightenment to reach fulfilment, which in turn is determined by the keen, middling, and tender quality of their factors maturing towards emancipation (*vimuttiparipācaniyā dhammā*).

Bodhisattvas also become threefold at the moment they form the aspiration, according to their division into those who comprehend through a condensed teaching (*ugghaṭitaññū*), those who comprehend through an elaborated teaching (*vipañcitaññū*), and those who are capable of training (*neyya*).[32] Among these, one who comprehends through a condensed teaching has such supporting conditions that, if he were disposed towards the enlightenment of a disciple, he could attain arahatship together with the four discriminations (*paṭisambhidā*) and the six direct knowledges while listening to a four-line stanza from the lips of a perfectly enlightened Buddha, even while the third line is as yet unconcluded. The second has such supporting conditions that, if he were disposed towards the enlightenment of a disciple, he could attain arahatship together with the six direct knowledges while listening to a four-line stanza from the lips of the Exalted One, even while the fourth line is as yet unconcluded. And the third has the supporting conditions to attain arahatship together with the six direct knowledges when the four-line stanza he hears from the Exalted One is concluded.

These three types, who form their aspirations without any allotted division of time, receive predictions (of their future Buddhahood) directly from the Buddhas. Then they fulfil the pāramīs in order and reach the supreme enlightenment according to the aforementioned time allotted to each type. But that these Great Beings, day by day giving great gifts like those given by Vessantara,[33] accumulating all the other pāramīs in the same way, making the five great relinquishings, reaching the summit in conduct for the good of kinsmen, conduct for the good of the world, and conduct developing intelligence—that they should become perfectly enlightened Buddhas before the time allotted to their respective types is fulfilled, this is not possible. Why? Because their knowledge is not yet mature enough and their accumulation of the factors issuing in Buddhahood not yet complete. For just as grain ripens only after the lapse of the time required (for its growth), so too the supreme enlightenment is perfected only after the lapse of the aforementioned periods of time. Before then, even though striving with all his might, the bodhisattva cannot attain enlightenment. The pāramīs are fulfilled according to the aforementioned distinction of time. Thus it should be understood.

(xv) WHAT BENEFITS DO THEY BRING?

The benefits obtained by bodhisattvas who have formed their aspirations are explained thus:

> Those men in all factors complete,
> Bound for perfect enlightenment,
> Though wandering through the round of births
> For countless aeons yet to come

> Never arise in Avīci hell,
> Nor in the intermundane voids.
> They never appear as titans black
> Or ghosts consumed by hunger and thirst.

Though reborn in the plane of pain,
They do not take on minor forms,
And when reborn in the human world
They never come deprived of sight.

Their hearing is intact from birth,
Nor are they dumb or lame of limb.
They never become of female sex,
Nor eunuchs or hermaphrodites.

Those men bound for enlightenment
Never commit the five black deeds.
Always pure in their way of life,
Their conduct's range is free from flaw.

They never hold perverted views
But recognize the kammic laws.
They are born at times in heavenly worlds,
But not in the mindless or pure abodes.

Those true men bent on renunciation,
Detached from all the planes of being,
Plough their course for the good of the world,
Striving to fulfil the pāramīs.

Some other benefits of the pāramīs are the following: The sixteen wonderful and marvellous qualities that begin: "Mindful and clearly comprehending, Ānanda, the bodhisattva passes away from the Tusita heaven and descends into his mother's womb" (D.ii,12); the thirty-two portents, such as "cold disappears and heat is allayed," and "when the bodhisattva is born, this ten thousandfold world-system shakes, trembles, and quakes," etc. (D.ii,15); and the other qualities shown here and there in the Jātakas, the Buddha-vaṁsa, etc., such as the fulfillment of the bodhisattva's wishes, his mastery over kamma, and so forth. Other benefits are the pairs of complementary qualities such as non-greed and non-hatred already discussed.

Moreover, from the time that he makes the aspiration, the bodhisattva becomes like a father to all beings, wishing for their welfare.

By reason of his distinguished qualities he is worthy of offerings, worthy of reverence, worthy of esteem, a supreme field of merit. He is generally dear to humans and to non-humans alike, and is protected by deities. Because his mind is grounded in loving-kindness and compassion, he cannot be harmed by wild beasts, etc. Whatever order of beings he is reborn in, on account of his distinguished merit, he surpasses the other beings there in his superior beauty, fame, happiness, strength, and dominion.

He is healthy and robust. His faith is very pure and lucid. His energy, mindfulness, concentration, and wisdom are also very pure and lucid. His defilements, disturbances, and passions are weak. Because his defilements are weak, he is easy to admonish, adroit, patient, meek, congenial and hospitable. He is free from anger, malice, denigration, domineering, envy, stinginess, craftiness, hypocrisy, obstinacy, pride, presumption and negligence. He endures torments at the hands of others but never torments anyone himself. Whenever he enters a village area, the unarisen dangers and calamities facing the beings there generally do not arise, and those which have arisen subside. And whenever he is reborn in the planes of misery, unlike the common inhabitants there he is not oppressed by excessive suffering but acquires an even greater sense of spiritual urgency.

Therefore these distinguished qualities of the Great Man—such as being like a father to beings, being worthy of offerings, etc.— found in this or that state of existence, are the benefits of the pāramīs.

Further, the accomplishment of life-span, the accomplishment of form, the accomplishment of family, the accomplishment of sovereignty, credibility, and greatness of spiritual power are also benefits of the Great Man's pāramīs. Therein, the "accomplishment of life-span" (*āyusampadā*) is length of life or longevity in whatever state of existence he takes rebirth in; by this means he concludes whatever wholesome undertakings he began and accumulates many wholesome qualities. The "accomplishment of form" (*rūpasampadā*) is beauty of form, comeliness, or loveliness; by this means he inspires confidence and esteem in beings who take physical form as their standard. The "accomplishment of family" (*kulasampadā*) is rebirth in excellent families; by this means he is (judged) to be worth approaching and ministering to by beings who are intoxicated with the vanity of birth, etc. The "accomplishment of sovereignty" (*issariyasampadā*) is greatness of power, greatness of influence, and greatness of retinue; by means of these he is able to benefit with the four bases of beneficence those who need to be benefited and to restrain with Dhamma those who need to be restrained. "Credibility" (*ādeyyavacanatā*) means trustworthiness, reliability; by this means he becomes an authority for beings, and his command cannot be disregarded. "Greatness of spiritual power" (*mahānubhāvatā*) means magnitude of spiritual power; by this means he cannot be vanquished by others, but he himself invariably vanquishes them— by Dhamma, by righteousness, and by his genuine noble qualities.

Thus the accomplishment of life-span and so forth are benefits of the Great Man's pāramīs. These are the causes for the growth of his own boundless requisites of merit, and the means by which he leads other beings to enter and reach maturity in the three vehicles.

(xvi) WHAT IS THEIR FRUIT?

Their fruit is, in brief, the state of perfect Buddhahood. In detail, it is the acquisition of the form-body (*rūpakāya*) resplendent with the multitude of meritorious qualities such as the thirty-two characteristics of a Great Man, the eighty minor marks of physical beauty, the fathom-wide aura, etc.; and, founded upon this, the glorious Dhamma-body (*dhammakāya*) radiant with its collection of infinite and boundless meritorious qualities—the ten powers, the four grounds of self-confidence, the six kinds of knowledge not held in common with others, the eighteen unique Buddha-qualities, and so forth.[34] And so numerous are the Buddha-qualities that even a perfectly enlightened Buddha could not finish describing them, even after many aeons. This is their fruit.

And it is said:

> If a Buddha were to speak in praise of a Buddha,
> Speaking nothing else for an aeon's length,
> Sooner would the long-standing aeon reach its end,
> But the praise of the Tathāgata would not reach its end.

Notes

1. *Taṇhāmānadiṭṭhīhi anupahatā karuṇūpāyakosallapariggahitā dānādayo guṇā pāramiyo.*

2. In Pāli: *dāna, sīla, nekkhamma, paññā, viriya, khanti, sacca, adhiṭṭhāna, mettā, upekkhā.* The passage is untraced, but see Buddhavaṁsa I, v.76.

3. An allusion to the first stage in the active career of a bodhisattva. After the bodhisattva makes his original aspiration at the feet of a living Buddha and receives from the latter the prediction of his future attainment of Buddhahood, he goes into solitude and investigates each of the pāramīs in terms of their specific characteristics. Following the investigation, he undertakes their practice. See Buddhavaṁsa II, vv.116-66.

4. The practice of giving brings as its kammic retribution the acquisition of wealth, the observance of precepts the attainment of a happy rebirth either in the heavens or in the human world.

5. Virtue, as the observance of precepts, prevents the transgression of moral principles by body and speech. Renunciation, as mental purification, removes the obsession with unwholesome qualities of mind.

6. *Dhammanijjhānakkhanti.* The word *khanti* is ordinarily used to mean patience in the sense of the forbearance of the wrongs of others and the endurance of hardships, but it is sometimes also used to signify the intellectual acceptance of doctrines which are not yet completely clear to the understanding. The compound *dhammanijjhānakkhanti* seems to indicate a stage in the growth of wisdom whereby the mind accepts intellectually principles initially assented to in faith without yet fully grasping them by immediate insight.

7. The requisites of enlightenment are the pāramīs themselves, divided into two groups: the requisites of merit (*puñña-*

sambhāra) and the requisites of knowledge (*ñāṇasambhāra*).

8.   The eight meditative attainments are the four jhānas and the four immaterial attainments. The five mundane direct knowledges are discussed briefly below, in the section on the practice of the perfection of wisdom. See p.51.

9.   *Kiṭṭaka.* None of the meanings in the standard dictionaries are relevant to the context.

10.   The first and lowest of the six sense-sphere heavens of Buddhist cosmology.

11.   Excluding the third noble truth, the cessation of suffering, which the bodhisattva will only realize directly upon his attainment of Buddhahood.

12.   For the four foundations, see below, pp.59-61; for the four bases, pp.64-65.

13.   *Anulomiyaṁ khantiyaṁ ṭhito.* "Acquiescence in conformity" indicates the stage in the development of insight where the meditator can accept the basic truths of his contemplation without yet having fully apprehended them by mature wisdom. See n.6.

14.   The seven stages of purification are mentioned in the Rathavinīta Sutta (M.24), and explained in detail in the *Visuddhimagga.* The "course of rightness" is the supramundane path leading to nibbāna; upon entering this course one becomes irreversibly bound for enlightenment and final deliverance. The three kinds of clear knowledge are the recollection of past lives, knowledge of the passing away and rebirth of beings, and knowledge of the destruction of the cankers. The five mundane direct knowledges are at p.51; the sixth is the knowledge of the destruction of the cankers. The four discriminations are the discrimination of meaning, of phenomena, of etymology, and of ingenuity (*attha, dhamma, nirutti, paṭibhāna*).

15.   The five eyes are the fleshly eye (*maṁsacakkhu*), the organ of physical sight, which for a Buddha is still many times

more powerful than the eyes of an ordinary man; the divine eye (*dibbacakkhu*), by which he sees beings pass away and re-arise in accordance with their kamma throughout all the planes of existence; the wisdom eye (*paññācakkhu*), by which he sees all phenomena in their specific and general characteristics and the modes of conditionality to which they are subject; the Buddha-eye (*buddhacakkhu*), by which he sees the propensities and dispositions of beings, as well as the maturity of their faculties; and the universal eye (*samantacakkhu*), his knowledge of omniscience.

16. The thirty-two major and eighty minor characteristics of a Great Man's body.

17. The four floods of sensual desire, desire for existence, wrong views, and ignorance.

18. The "three times" are before presenting the gift, while giving it, and after giving it.

19. On the subject of the *vāsanā* or "mental impressions" the commentary to the Udāna says: "The *vāsanā* are particular dispositions to actions existing as a mere potential force built up through the defilements that have been brought into play through the course of beginningless time. Found in the mental continua even of those who are devoid of defilements (i.e. of arahats), they function as springs for conduct similar to the conduct followed while the defilements were yet unabandoned. In the case of the Exalted Buddhas, who through the fulfilment of their original aspiration abandon the defilements along with the obstruction of the knowable, no *vāsanā* remain in their mental continuities. But in the case of disciple-arahats and paccekabuddhas, who abandon the defilements without removing the obstruction of the knowable, the *vāsanā* remain." The classical example of this is the case of the Venerable Pilindavaccha who, though an arahat, continued to address other bhikkhus by the word *vasala*, a derogatory term used by brahmins to refer to those of low

caste. This bhikkhu, however, did not use the word due to conceit or contempt for others, both of which defilements he had utterly destroyed, but merely through the habitual force of past usage, since he had been a brahmin through many previous lives. See Ud.III,6 and its commentary.

20. The eight qualities of the Buddha's voice: it is frank, clear, melodious, pleasant, full, carrying, deep and resonant, and does not travel beyond his audience.

21. The four ariyan traditions (*ariyavaṁsa*) are contentment with any kind of robe, almsfood, and dwelling, and delight in meditation.

22. For the mundane kinds of full understanding (*pariññā*) see Vism.XX,3-5. The specific characteristics are the defining marks of each particular type of phenomena, the general characteristics their common marks of impermanence, suffering, and non-self. The preliminary portion of the wisdom born of meditation is comprised under the mundane kinds of full understanding. According to the Theravāda account, a bodhisattva cannot attain the supramundane wisdom until the eve of his enlightenment, for he must wait until his pāramis have reached the level of completeness required for Buddhahood before entering the path to final deliverance.

23. The knowledge of kammic retribution (also called knowledge of the passing away and re-arising of beings) and the knowledge of the future are two accessories of the divine eye; thus, though seven items are listed, only five direct knowledges are involved. The sixth is the knowledge of the destruction of the cankers, the attainment of arahatship.

24. For the five *abhiññā*, see Vism.XII-XIII; for the sphere of wisdom, XIV-XVII; for the five purifications of wisdom, XVIII-XXII.

25. Purification by knowledge and vision is the supramundane wisdom of the four noble paths. Because this purification issues in the realization of nibbāna, the bodhisattva-aspirant

must stop short of this attainment so that his realization of nibbāna will coincide with his perfect enlightenment.

26. An allusion to the pāramīs of energy, patience, and truthfulness.

27. The four paths, the four fruits, and nibbāna.

28. This is the standard enumeration of the *pāramitās* in the Mahāyāna literature, though the list itself probably goes back to the pre-Mahāyāna schools.

29. Perhaps giving fearlessness through observing the precepts, and giving the Dhamma through wisdom.

30. See M.iii,240-46, where the four foundations are explained in relation to arahatship.

31. The duration of a great aeon is indicated in the texts only by means of similes, e.g. if there were a mountain crag of solid granite a *yojana* (7 miles) high and a *yojana* round, and a man passing it once every hundred years were to stroke it once with a silk hankerchief, by this means it would take less time for him to wear away the mountain than it takes for an aeon to elapse. An "incalculable" means an incalculable number of great aeons; it must be distinguished from the four incalculables which make up each great aeon, the four periods of expansion, evolution, contraction, and dissolution.

32. The suttanta basis for this classification is found at A.ii,135.

33. The last human existence of the bodhisattva who became the Buddha Gotama, a prince noted for his generosity and selflessness.

34. Although the concept of the Dharmakāya came, in Mahāyāna Buddhism, to acquire a distinct ontological sense, as expressing the metaphysical identity of the Buddha's essential nature with the totality of particular existents, here the term *dhammakāya* is used simply to signify the collection of spiritual qualities which define the nature of a Buddha, without any ontological implications.

THE BUDDHIST PUBLICATION SOCIETY

The BPS is an approved charity dedicated to making known the Teaching of the Buddha, which has a vital message for people of all creeds. Founded in 1958, the BPS has published a wide variety of books and booklets covering a great range of topics. Its publications include accurate annotated translations of the Buddha's discourses, standard reference works, as well as original contemporary expositions of Buddhist thought and practice. These works present Buddhism as it truly is—a dynamic force which has influenced receptive minds for the past 2500 years and is still as relevant today as it was when it first arose. A full list of our publications will be sent upon request with an enclosure of U.S. $1.50 or its equivalent to cover air mail postage. Write to:

The Hony. Secretary
BUDDHIST PUBLICATION SOCIETY
P.O. Box 61
54, Sangharaja Mawatha
Kandy • Sri Lanka